THE EMERGENT EXECUTIVE: A DYNAMIC FIELD THEORY OF THE DEVELOPMENT OF EXECUTIVE FUNCTION

EDITED BY

Aaron T. Buss and John P. Spencer
University of Iowa
Department of Psychology and Delta Center

WITH COMMENTARY BY

Sandra A. Wiebe and J. Bruce Morton

Patricia J. Bauer
Series Editor

MONOGRAPHS OF THE SOCIETY FOR RESEARCH IN CHILD DEVELOPMENT

Serial No. 313, Vol. 79, No. 2, 2014

WILEY   *Boston, Massachusetts*   *Oxford, United Kingdom*

THE EMERGENT EXECUTIVE: A DYNAMIC FIELD THEORY OF THE DEVELOPMENT OF EXECUTIVE FUNCTION

CONTENTS

COMMENTARY

ABSTRACT

Executive function (EF) is a central aspect of cognition that undergoes significant changes in early childhood. Changes in EF in early childhood are robustly predictive of academic achievement and general quality of life measures later in adulthood. We present a dynamic neural field (DNF) model that provides a process-based account of behavior and developmental change in a key task used to probe the early development of executive function—the Dimensional Change Card Sort (DCCS) task. In the DCCS, children must flexibly switch from sorting cards either by shape or color to sorting by the other dimension. Typically, 3-year-olds, but not 5-year-olds, lack the flexibility to do so and perseverate on the first set of rules when instructed to switch. Using the DNF model, we demonstrate how rule-use and behavioral flexibility come about through a form of dimensional attention. Further, developmental change is captured by increasing the robustness and precision of dimensional attention. Note that although this enables the model to effectively switch tasks, the dimensional attention system does not "know" the details of task-specific performance. Rather, correct performance emerges as a property of system–wide interactions. We show how this captures children's behavior in quantitative detail across 14 versions of the DCCS task. Moreover, we successfully test a set of novel predictions with 3-year-old children from a version of the task not explained by other theories.

I. THE EMERGENCE OF EXECUTIVE FUNCTION

Early childhood is a time of rapid change in the organization of cognition. The period between 2 and 5 years is particularly dramatic, including the transition into formal schooling, the acquisition of language and mathematical abilities, learning to take the perspective of others in social interactions, and learning to appropriately adapt behavior across different contexts (e.g., Bull & Scerif, 2001; Frye, Zelazo, & Palfai, 1995; Kochanska, Coy, & Murray, 2001; Mazocco & Kover, 2007; Samuelson & Smith, 1999; Zelazo, Müller, Frye, & Marcovitch, 2003). This developmental period is also marked by dramatic changes in executive function (EF). EF is an umbrella term that refers to the processes that allow individuals to rise above the exigencies of the environment, habits, or internally prepotent behaviors to behave in a contextually appropriate and goal-driven manner.

EF is an important topic of study in early childhood because it has widespread influences on the organization of behavior and behavioral control. For instance, improvements in EF have a positive impact on language development, and deficits in executive control have been linked to specific language impairment (Im-Bolter, Johnson, & Pascual-Leone, 2006; McEvoy, Rodgers, & Pennington, 1993). Further, high levels of EF confer an initial advantage in mathematical and reading proficiency that has a facilitative effect on development through the early school years (Bull & Scerif, 2001; Mazocco & Kover, 2007). Aspects of EF have also been linked to theory of mind and perspective taking, which require children to suppress their own perspective and adopt the perspective of others (Carlson, Moses, & Breton, 2002; Frye et al., 1995; Hughes & Ensor, 2007). Finally, children with ADHD and autism show deficits in all three components of EF discussed below, displaying weaker inhibitory control, a poorer ability to maintain information in working memory (WM), and greater difficulty switching tasks (Corbett, Constantine, Hendren, Rocke, & Ozonoff, 2009; Geurts, Verté, Oosterlaan, Roeyers, & Sergeant, 2004; Happé, Booth, Charlton, & Hughes, 2006; McEvoy et al., 1993; Pennington & Ozonoff, 1996). The exact role of EF deficits in these pathologies, however, remains debated (Liss et al., 2001).

Critically, individual differences in EF early in development can produce long-lasting effects. Data show that enhancing EFs in early development can enhance school performance and reduce the prevalence of psychopathology (see Diamond & Lee, 2011; Liss et al., 2001; Pennington & Ozonoff, 1996). Indeed, data suggest that EFs are more important for school readiness than IQ (Blair & Razza, 2007), in part, because EFs predict math and reading competence throughout the school years (Gathercole, Pickering, Knight, & Stegmann, 2004). EFs remain important into adulthood, predicting career and marriage satisfaction and positive mental and physical health (Dunn, 2010; Eakin et al., 2004; Prince et al., 2007). Reversely, children 3–11 years with poorer EFs have worse health, earn less, and commit more crimes as adults, even when controlling for IQ, gender, and social class (Moffitt et al., 2011).

Early theories of EF proposed that the emergence of cognitive flexibility reflected developmental changes in a central executive system—a central resource that controls other aspects of cognition (Baddeley, 1986; Duncan, Emslie, Williams, Johnson, & Freer, 1996; Duncan, Johnson, Swales, & Freer, 1997; Norman & Shallice, 1986). This view was anchored, in part, to evidence that core executive functions could be localized to lateral pre-frontal cortex, a large region anterior to the precentral sulcus. Lateral pre-frontal cortex is one of the slowest developing brain regions (Giedd et al., 1999) and evidence from patient populations (Baddeley, Della Salla, Papagno, & Spinnler, 1997; Milner, 1963) and single-unit neurophysiology (Asaad, Rainer, & Miller, 2000; Rao, Rainer, & Miller, 1997) showed that impairments of PFC leads to behaviors that mimic the performance of young children (Dempster, 1992; Diamond, 2002).

Factor analytic models suggest, however, that cognitive control and flexibility do not reflect the operation of a single resource. Rather, EF has multiple distinct components. Generally, EF is thought to involve the *inhibition* or suppression of irrelevant information or inappropriate actions, the stable maintenance or representation of information in *working memory* over time in a way that prevents interference or distraction, and the flexible updating or *switching* of cognitive processes to meet new goals (Collette et al., 2005; Davidson, Amso, Anderson, & Diamond, 2006; Garon, Bryson, & Smith, 2008; Lehto, Juujärvi, Kooistra, & Pulkkinen, 2003; Miyake, Friedman, Emerson, Witzki, & Howerter, 2000). Factor analytic approaches have supported this multi-component view of EF, showing that different EF tasks load on inhibition, working memory, and task switching in different ways (Huizinga, Dolan, & van der Molen, 2006; Lehto et al., 2003; Miyake et al., 2000; however, see Wiebe et al., 2011). We organize our review of the development of EF below based on these three component processes. Note that we use these labels simply to distinguish different aspects of functionality that executive control achieves (see Zelazo et al., 2003), rather than making strong claims that these processes capture all aspects of EF. Ultimately, the real challenge in explaining EF is to understand the numerous ways cognitive

2

control can emerge in specific tasks from a complex, multi-component system.

The multi-component nature of EF revealed by behavioral studies is also reflected in neural evidence. Data from neuroimaging studies has shown an extensive network of regions within frontal and posterior cortical areas that are involved in EF (for review, see Courtney, 2004; Dosenbach et al., 2007; Fair et al., 2007, 2008; Morton, 2010; Postle, 2006). Cognitive control and flexibility are thought to emerge from interactions within this system-wide network. One useful tool in understanding the neural basis of EF is resting state connectivity analysis, in which the endogenous fluctuations in baseline activity are correlated across voxels to reveal functionally connected regions. Fair and coworkers (Dosenbach et al., 2007; Fair et al., 2007, 2009) have used this approach to identify distinct networks involved in different aspects of cognitive control. One network is composed of frontoparietal connections across regions such as dorsolateral prefrontal cortex, intraparietal sulcus, and precuneus. This network is hypothesized to be involved in trial-to-trial adaptation, task-initiation, and error adjustment. The other network is composed of cinguloopercular connections across regions thought to be involved in the stable maintenance of task-sets, including anterior prefrontal cortex, anterior cingulate cortex, anterior insula, and ventral prefrontal cortex, along with sensory areas in occipital and temporal cortex (Dosenbach et al., 2007).

Although neuroimaging data have shed important light on the neural systems involved in EF, they have also revealed new complexities. For instance, it is not clear how the different component processes of EF identified in the behavioral literature map onto the functional networks identified using neuroimaging techniques. The story gets even more complex when we look at development. Here, we see that each component process of EF has its own developmental trajectory with complex interactions among the processes. Moreover, the neural systems involved in EF change dramatically over development.

The Development of EF: Behavioral Evidence

The different component processes of EF—inhibition, working memory, and task switching—emerge in task-specific contexts at different points during early childhood. Response inhibition develops in a rudimentary form late in infancy as indexed by the A-not-B task (Marcovitch & Zelazo, 1999; Thelen, Schöner, Scheier, & Smith, 2001). In this task, children build up a habit of reaching to one location (the A location), and are then cued to reach to a new location (the B location). Typically, infants younger than 10 months cannot inhibit the prepotent response to reach to A and continue to reach to that location when cued to reach to the B location. By 10–12 months, infants

3

succeed in the canonical task. By 3 years, more complex tasks can be used to study inhibitory processes that pit internalized, abstract rules against prepotent behaviors. Many of these tasks resemble tasks used with adults, including child versions of Go/No-go (Cragg & Nation, 2008; Dowsett & Livsey, 2000), Stroop (Carlson, 2005), Simon (Gerardi-Caulton, 2000), and flanker tasks (Rueda et al., 2004). In these studies, a stimulus primes a response that is either compatible or incompatible with current task demands. On incompatible trials, children show robust deficits that diminish from ages 3 to 5 (Dowsett & Livsey, 2000; Gerardi-Caulton, 2000).

Working memory involves the active maintenance of information or goals over a brief period of time in the service of a particular task. A critical aspect of developmental change in working memory is an increase in capacity, or the amount of information that can be actively maintained simultaneously. Capacity shows improvements between 3 and 5 years (Isaacs & Vargha-Khadem, 1989; Logie & Pearson, 1997; Simmering, 2008), and continues to increase into childhood and adolescence (Cowan et al., 2005; Isaacs & Vargha-Khadem, 1989; Logie & Pearson, 1997; Simmering, 2008; Vicari, Bellucci, & Carlesimo, 2003). One limitation of this research is that it can be difficult to tease apart capacity limits from other aspects of task performance such as rehearsal and chunking (Dempster, 1981; Pickering, 2001; Simmering, 2011). To overcome this limitation, researchers examining one type of working memory—visual working memory (VWM)—have used the change detection task (Luck & Vogel, 1997), which uses novel objects and short memory delays to control the influence of rehearsal and other strategic influences. Use of this task has revealed increases from a capacity of 1–2 items at 3 years to 3 items at 5 years to 4–5 items at 10 years (Isaacs & Vargha-Khadem, 1989; Logie & Pearson, 1997; Simmering, 2012; Vicari et al., 2003).

Finally, task switching begins to emerge around 2 years of age. This process is typically assessed by having participants switch from using one set of rules or goals (e.g., sort by color) to using another (e.g., sort by shape). At 2 years of age, children can reliably engage a single rule to guide behavior, but perseveratively use only one rule if the task contains more (Zelazo, Reznick, & Piñon, 1995). At this age, then, children have difficulty implementing a rule-set that requires choosing from alternate responses. Switching from one rule set to another is possible in some tasks at 3 years of age (Brace, Morton, & Munakata, 2006; Fisher, 2011; Müller, Dick, Gela, Overton, & Zelazo, 2006; Zelazo et al., 2003), for example, if the two rule-pairs are univalent (associated with different stimuli). It is not until 5 years of age, however, that children can reliably switch from one rule set to another using the same stimulus set (Müller et al., 2006; Zelazo et al., 2003). Importantly, switch costs, as indexed by reaction times, are still seen throughout childhood, adolescence, and adulthood (Diamond & Kirkham, 2005; Morton, Bosma, & Ansari, 2009).

In summary, there are dramatic changes in each component process of EF between 12 months and 5 years. Moreover, these components change in task-specific ways that are protracted throughout early childhood. For instance, the early emergence of inhibitory control can be probed in the A-not-B task in infancy, but related changes in inhibitory control do not emerge in the Go/No-go task until 3–5 years. Less well studied is how changes in one component process impact the other processes, and how children harness and integrate these processes to show robust cognitive control and flexibility by 5 years. In the next section, we turn to neural evidence from developmental studies of EF. Results from this literature reveal an equally complex picture.

The Development of EF: Neural Evidence

EF undergoes critical changes between 12 months and 5 years. This creates challenges for efforts to understand the neural bases of EF given that use of fMRI is difficult in this age range. Three main approaches have been used to overcome these challenges.

The first approach has used fMRI to examine anatomical and functional connectivity changes in brain activity related to EF in older children and adolescents. These studies have revealed a strengthening of long range connections that serve to integrate components of the functional networks involved in EF and segregate the networks form one another (Fair et al., 2009). For instance, Hwang, Velanova, and Luna (2010) reported an increase in connectivity between frontal and parietal areas along with a decrease in connectivity within parietal cortex in a study of 8- to 12-year-olds, 13- to 17-year-olds, and 18- to 27-year-olds. Thus, emerging control is supported by strengthening interactions between frontal and parietal areas.

Other studies have shown extensive changes to EF networks over development, including changes in cortical volume, structural differentiation, and the dynamics of neural activation (Barnea-Goraly et al., 2005; Crone, Donohue, Honomichl, Wendelken, & Bunge, 2006; Fair et al., 2007; Gogtay et al., 2004; Kelly et al., 2009; Lenroot & Giedd, 2006; Moriguchi & Hiraki, 2009; Sowell, Trauner, Gamst, & Jernigan, 2002; Stevens, Pearlson, & Calhoun, 2009; Stevens, Skudlarski, Pearlson, & Calhoun, 2009; Tsujimoto, 2008). Thus, the emergence of EF does not reflect changes in a single area of the brain, but instead reflects the development and organization of neural structures throughout the brain.

Two other approaches to studying the development of EF have focused on measuring functional activity as children engage in specific tasks that load on different component processes of EF. One of these approaches uses fMRI and studies the behavior of older children and adolescents. The second approach uses functional Near-Infrared Spectroscopy (fNIRS) with young children. fNIRS measures changes in cortical hemodynamics using the optical properties of oxygenated- and deoxygenated-hemoglobin (Cui, Bray, Bryant, Glover, & Reiss, 2011; Minati, Visani, Dowell, Medford, & Critchley, 2011). Thus, as with fMRI, fNIRS provides a localized hemodynamic measure that reflects active cognitive processing in cortex. However, in contrast to fMRI, fNIRS is much quieter and much more resistant to artifacts created by motion. Thus, fNIRS is more readily adaptable for use with very young children and infants. In the sections that follow, we review these two neuroimaging approaches to the development of EF, again organized by EF component processes.

Inhibition

Baird et al. (2002) recorded fNIRS from frontal cortex while infants performed the A-not-B task. These researchers reported an increase in frontal activation associated with correct reaching to the B location. Thus, inhibiting motor habits, even at this early age, recruits regions of frontal cortex. Similarly, Schroeter, Zysset, Wahl, and von Cramon (2004) recorded fNIRS while 7- to 13-year-olds performed a Stroop task and found increased activity in left lateral prefrontal cortex associated with greater inhibitory control.

Similar results have been reported using fMRI. Durston et al. (2002) compared go-no-go performance and associated fMRI data between a group of 6- to 10-year-olds and adults. Adults were both faster and more accurate on "go" trials, but both age groups showed stronger activation on "no-go" trials in ventral prefrontal cortex (PFC) bilaterally, right dorsolateral PFC, and right parietal cortex. Thus, greater inhibitory demands are associated with stronger neural activation. This reveals an important distinction between cognitive constructs and neural measures: although inhibition is associated with a suppression of behavior, it is nonetheless supported by an increase in neural activation. As we discuss later, computational models can play an important role in clarifying such distinctions between behavioral and neural processes.

Working Memory

Thomason et al. (2009) studied a group of 7- to 12-year-olds and adults with fMRI and found that activation in frontal and parietal regions scaled with the number of items to be remembered. Further, this study found left lateralization for verbal WM but right lateralization for spatial WM. Tsujii, Yamamoto, Masuda, and Watanabe (2009) used fNIRS to examine spatial WM with 5- and 7-year-olds and found that 5-year-olds did not show lateralized specialization of frontal cortex while 7-year-olds did show this pattern. Thus, the lateralization of spatial WM emerges early in childhood.

Klingberg, Forssberg, and Westerberg (2002) reported stronger superior frontal and intraparietal cortex activity with increasing WM capacity between 9 and 18 years. Edin, Macoveanu, Olesen, Tengér, and Klingberg (2007)

6

further showed that stronger fronto-parietal connectivity is associated with improvements in WM (see also, Edin et al., 2009). Thus, over development the fronto-parietal network supporting visual WM is established and becomes increasingly sensitive to the size of the WM load. Note, further, that the neural basis of WM and inhibitory control share many aspects. For instance, McNab et al. (2008) compared neural activation associated with visual WM and inhibitory control and found common patterns of activation in right inferior and middle frontal cortex, as well as right parietal areas.

Task Switching

Different lines of fMRI data have revealed dissociable components of rule-switching in tasks that only require shifting of responses versus shifting of attention (e.g., Nagahama et al., 2001). With adults, the ventro-lateral prefrontal cortex and rostro-lateral prefrontal cortex are more active when demands on rule-representation are high (i.e., when sets of response mappings conflict with one another), while the supplementary- and pre-supplementary motor areas together with the basal ganglia are more active when switching rules or reconfiguring a rule-set (Crone, Wendelken, Donohue, & Bunge, 2006; for a review of the neural circuitry underlying rule-use, see Bunge, 2004; Bunge et al., 2005).

Critically, research has revealed differences in these neural dynamics over development. Specifically, 8- to 12-year-olds display a less-differentiated pattern of neural activation than adults. These children engage the pre-supplementary motor area for rule-representation, not simply rule-switching as with adults. Further, while adults show heightened ventro-lateral pre-frontal cortex activation for bivalent rules on both rule-repeat and rule-switch trials, children show greater activation in this area for both univalent rules and switch trials (Crone, Donohue, et al., 2006).

Making Sense of Complexity: Computational Modeling Offers a Way Forward

Our survey of the literature on the development of EF paints a complicated picture. On one hand, data showing that improvements in EF early in development can have a long-lasting impact on behavioral functioning makes the study of EF during this time period critically important. On the other hand, it is not clear how to integrate the complex pattern of behavioral and neural findings from the literature into a cohesive theoretical account.

It is clear from the literature, however, that a theory of the early development of EF must tackle several fundamental challenges. First, explaining the emergence of EF requires that we understand how each component process changes over development. Next, we must understand how changes in one process at one point in time relate to changes in the other processes at later points in time. Third, the rich neural picture that has emerged in the EF literature suggests that we need theories that can bridge the gap between behavioral and neural systems. Fourth, theories of EF must integrate processes over multiple timescales: in the moment as cognitive control is executed within a trial, over the course of learning as EF is facilitated or impaired over experience with particular tasks, and over development as new behaviors are realized and flexibly employed in the service of task goals. Finally, theories of EF must grapple with the central challenge of autonomy: how can a system control and change itself autonomously, that is, without an explicit controller or homunculus?

Different theories of EF have tackled different subsets of these challenges. For instance, models of EF in adults have focused on capturing behavior during individual trials and how performance changes over learning (Anderson, 1993; Meyer & Kieras, 1997; O'Reilly, Braver, & Cohen, 1999). Developmental models, by contrast, have focused more on changes in EF across months and years during infancy and early childhood (Marcovitch & Zelazo, 2009; Morton & Munakata, 2002; Zelazo et al., 2003). And several models have tried to bridge the gap between brain and behavior, capturing behavioral data using neurally grounded models that mimic properties of cortical and sub-cortical neural systems (Herd, Banich, & O'Reilly, 2003; O'Reilly & Frank, 2006).

In our view, this latter class of models offers a particularly compelling approach to understanding the early development of EF given the long history of considering executive control from both a behavioral and neural perspective. For instance, this class of models can help us understand how neural processes are functionally related to cognition (Ashby & Waldschmidt, 2008), that is, how neural processes distributed across a network of regions can give rise to the behavioral characteristics measured in working memory and response inhibition tasks. Concretely, specific neural processes can be implemented in a neural network model. Then, the model's overt behavior can be compared to empirical findings, while the model's simulated neural dynamics can be compared to neural data. In this way, the computational model can serve as a bridge to understand the link between neural dynamics and cognitive processes (for a discussion of this approach to cognitive neuroscience, see Ashby & Waldschmidt, 2008; Forstmann, Wagenmakers, Eichele, Brown, & Serences, 2011; also see Behrens, Woolrich, Walton, & Rushworth, 2007; Friston, 2009; Pessiglione, Seymour, Flandin, Dolan, & Frith, 2009).

The success of several examples using this method is promising. For example, Deco and Rolls (2004; see also, Deco & Rolls, 2005) implemented an integrate-and-fire neural network that produced realistic neuronal spiking dynamics. The model was used to simulate versions of spatial and object working memory tasks used with adults. Moreover, the researchers developed a method to link neural activity in the model directly to the BOLD response measured with fMRI (based on studies of the neural basis of the BOLD signal; see Logothetis, Pauls, Augath, Trinath, & Oeltermann, 2001). Using this method, Deco and Rolls were able to reproduce hemodynamic data from different parts of pre-frontal cortex. This led the authors to speculate about the functional role of pre-frontal cortex in working memory and the different inhibitory processes that might play out in different regions of pre-frontal cortex. Further, Edin et al. (2007) used a similar model to simulate developmental changes in working memory capacity. These researchers used the model to test out different hypotheses about how neural interactions might change over development. Simulated data showed that strengthening fronto-parietal connections for units coding for similar values in the model produced the best fit of hemodynamic and behavioral data during later childhood.

Toward a Neural Dynamic Theory of the Development of EF

In the present report, we propose a new theory of the early development of executive function using the framework of Dynamic Field Theory (DFT). DFT uses simulated real-time neural population dynamics within artificial cortical fields to capture the processes hypothesized to underlie behavioral decisions in-the-moment, as well as how neural processes change over learning and development (for reviews, see Schöner, 2009; Spencer, Perone, & Johnson, 2009). This approach is well-positioned to tackle the complexity of EF in early development. In particular, DFT has been used to examine the early emergence of response inhibition in the context of the A-not-B error (Smith, Thelen, Titzer, & McLin, 1999; Thelen et al., 2001), as well as response selection processes later in development (Erlhagen & Schöner, 2002). Similarly, DFT has been used to explain changes in visual working memory capacity in early development (Simmering, 2008) and how the mechanisms that underlie working memory lead to counterintuitive behavioral findings with adults (Johnson, Spencer, Luck & Schöner, 2009). Further, DFT has been used to probe task-switching processes in the context of dual-task performance with adults (Buss, Wifall, Hazeltine, & Spencer, 2014).

DFT also provides a bridge between behavioral processes and neural measures. For instance, Schöner, Erlhagen, and coworkers have developed an approach to directly link simulated activation dynamics in neural field models to single- and multi-unit neurophysiology (Erlhagen, Bastian, Jancke, Riehle, & Schöner, 1999; Jancke et al., 1999), enabling researchers to test a theory of response preparation both behaviorally and neurally with non-human primates (Bastian, Riehle, Erlhagen, & Schöner, 1998; Bastian, Schöner, & Riehle, 2003). This approach has also been extended to studies of visual cortical processing using voltage-sensitive dye imaging (Markounikau, Igel, Grinvald, & Jancke, 2010). Finally, several studies have probed the link between DFT and ERP measures with humans, testing dynamic neural field accounts of motor planning (McDowell, Jeka, Schöner, & Hatfield, 2002) and multi-object tracking (Spencer, Barich, Goldberg, & Perone, 2012).

Given the complexity of the literature on the early development of EF, we anchor our theoretical account to data from a particular task that provides a common frame of reference for understanding changes in EF—the Dimensional Change Card Sort (DCCS) task. This is a switching task that also involves aspects of inhibition and working memory, making it an ideal probe of EF in early development (Carlson, 2005; Waxer & Morton, 2011; see Garon et al., 2008). Moreover, the rate of perseverative errors in early childhood is predictive of later functioning (Biederman et al., 2007; Hughes & Ensor, 2007; Ozonoff & McEvoy, 1994; Schneider, Lockl, & Fernandez, 2005). Finally, the vast literature using the DCCS task provides robust constraints for a developmental theory.

Although we focus on the DCCS task in the present report, the work presented here provides a critical step toward a general theory of the development of EF. In particular, the model we present implements a distributed network of simulated cortical fields that display aspects of EF through neural interactions within the network. This provides a framework for thinking about brain-behavior links in early development. We explore this link initially by asking how, for instance, response inhibition—a behavioral construct—is related to simulated neural processes in our model. Here, we will discuss how "inhibition" stems from robust neural activation in the model and how this construct is related to working memory processes (for related ideas, see Morton & Munakata, 2002; Roberts, Hager, & Herron, 1994; Roberts & Pennington, 1996; Stedron, Sahni, & Munakata, 2005). The model also provides a platform for testing out specific developmental hypotheses, and how neuro-developmental mechanisms can give rise to the behavioral changes reported in the literature between 3 and 5 years. We will also consider how the simulated neural processes in our model related to EF measures from other tasks, as well as neural measures from the fMRI/fNIRS literature. Finally, in the General Discussion in Chapter VII, we will pull back to the most general level and ask what our theory might say about EF beyond the laboratory. That is, we discuss whether our theory sheds light on how EF changes over development in the real world and how we might intervene in future work to facilitate the development of EF.

The remainder of this monograph is divided into six chapters. In the next chapter, we review the literature on the DCCS task, including theories that account for different aspects of children's performance. In Chapter III, we describe a dynamic field theory of executive function and how this theory captures performance in the standard version of the DCCS task. We also consider how this theory relates to EF processes more generally. In Chapter IV, we probe the ability of the model to move beyond current theories by quantitatively simulating children's performance from multiple variants of the DCCS task. In Chapter V, we generate and test novel predictions regarding the role of spatial locations in feature binding in the DCCS task. Importantly, data from this study are not consistent with any other theory of the early development of EF. In Chapter VI, we present further simulation results highlighting the ability of the model to capture asymmetrical switch costs associated with different attentional manipulations in the DCCS task. Finally, in Chapter VII we contrast the DFT with other theories in the literature as well as evaluate the strengths and limitations of this theoretical approach to the emergence of EF in early development. We conclude by discussing prospects for future work that seeks to understand the early organization of EF at the behavioral and neural levels as well as how EF develops autonomously outside of the laboratory.

II. A CASE STUDY OF THE DCCS TASK

The DCCS task has been extensively used over the last two decades to probe the development of cognitive flexibility in early childhood. Given the important and predictive role EF plays in early childhood (see Blair & Razza, 2007; Diamond & Lee, 2011; Gathercole et al., 2004; Liss et al., 2001; Moffitt et al., 2011; Pennington & Ozonoff, 1996), this task provides an ideal starting point to develop a neural process account of EF. In this task, children are instructed to switch from sorting cards based on shape or color to sorting based on the other dimension using verbal rules provided by the experimenter (e.g., "Sort by shape/Sort by color"). Trays mark two sorting locations where target cards are affixed. These target cards provide cues as to which features go where (e.g., a blue-circle and a red-star). The test cards that children sort are typically constructed so that they match either target card along one dimension (e.g., a blue-star and a red-circle; see Figure 1A). Thus, there is direct conflict when making a decision for a given card since it could go to either location depending on the dimension used for sorting.

The DCCS is an ideal task to study the early development of EF for three reasons. First, performance in the DCCS involves not only "switching," but also builds upon "inhibition" and "working memory," which develop in some forms before flexible rule-use (Carlson, 2005; Garon et al., 2008). In particular, this task requires inhibition to suppress processing of the irrelevant dimension, working memory to maintain representations of the relevant task rules, and task switching in order to update these processes after the rule-switch (Garon et al., 2008). Further, ERP data suggest that multiple control processes unfold over the course of a trial, suggesting that the task does not tap into only a switching component (Waxer & Morton, 2011). Thus, flexible rule-use in this context taps into multiple aspects of EF.

Second, this task reveals rapid and dramatic changes in children's executive function in early development. Although 5-year-olds have little trouble switching rules, the majority of 3-year-olds (typically around 70%) perseverates and continues using the first set of rules after they are instructed to switch. This perseveration is robust and persists despite constant reminders that the rules have changed. The dramatic nature of this developmental shift has led to an intensive investigation of why young children perseverate,

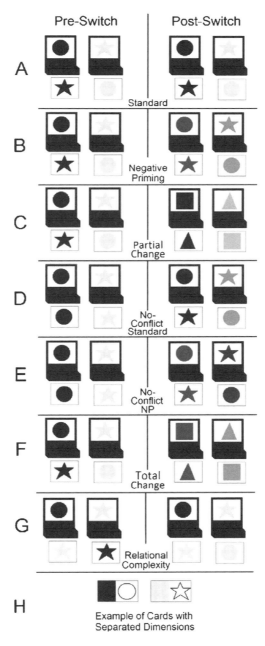

FIGURE 1.—Target and test cards used in various versions of the Dimensional Change Card Sort (DCCS). For all of the examples shown *color* is the pre-shape dimension and *shape* is the post-switch dimension.

creating a vast literature on the DCCS task. This literature has revealed complex and subtle aspects of children's rule-use, explaining why single-cause explanations (e.g., inhibitory control) fall short of capturing the full range of behavioral effects and why a formal, computational approach is warranted. Simply put, children fail to switch rules in very specific ways, and a successful integrative theory must capture these details. For example, 3-year-olds do not have trouble using the initial set of rules. Rather, difficulty only arises in particular circumstances during the post-switch phase. Further, children's post-switch performance is typically all-or-none—that is, they either get all of the trials correct or all of the trials incorrect. In addition, although perseveration is robust in many variants of the task, 3-year-olds are able to switch rules under specific conditions. Ultimately, the pattern of success and failure across different manipulations reveal critical details that a theory must capture.

The third reason why the DCCS task provides an ideal foundation for developing a theory of EF harkens back to the long history of trying to integrate behavioral and neural data in the EF literature. In addition to a rich behavioral data set in the DCCS literature, there is an emerging neuroimaging literature that has shown rapid and dramatic changes in children's neural dynamics in early development. This work has revealed changes in a network of brain areas associated with rule-switching which emerges after age 3 and becomes more refined into adulthood (Moriguchi & Hiraki, 2009; Morton et al., 2009). Thus, this simple task can provide insight to the wide spectrum of EF processes *and* associated neural changes in early childhood.

Below, we review the literature on the DCCS task, starting with a review of behavioral studies organized around the different components of executive function as well as other themes highlighted in the literature. We then discuss neuroimaging studies on the early development of EF. Finally, we survey existing theories of the DCCS task. This survey reveals several strengths of existing accounts, but also key limitations that lay the foundation for the Dynamic Field Theory (DFT) we present in Chapter 3.

Review of Behavioral Studies

The Role of Inhibition

Several studies have probed the role that inhibitory processes play in children's perseveration in the DCCS task. This has been accomplished by altering different features of the target and test cards between the pre- and post-switch phases. These data show that children do not perseverate based on a fixed set of features or rules; rather, the dimensions and features on the cards participate in a more subtle pattern of interactions.

In a Negative Priming version, the features that were *relevant* for the pre-switch phase (e.g., color) are changed for the post-switch phase (e.g., shape;

14

see Figure 1B). With the pre-switch features changed, the stimuli no longer afford being sorted by the color values used during the pre-switch phase; thus, it is not required that children inhibit those values or rules during the post-switch phase. However, around 60% of 3-year-olds fail to switch rules in this version suggesting they have difficulty overcoming the negative priming that occurs as the irrelevant features are ignored or suppressed during the pre-switch phase (Müller et al., 2006; Zelazo et al., 2003). That is, 3-year-olds appear to have too much inhibition of the post-switch dimension that they cannot overcome. In a Partial-Change version (Zelazo et al., 2003), the reverse issue is probed, that is, the features that were *irrelevant* during the pre-switch are changed in the post-switch phase (see Figure 1C). With these features changed, the rules for the post-switch feature values would not be negatively primed going into the post-switch. Nevertheless, more than half of 3-year-olds also have difficulty switching in this task presumably due to their inability to inhibit the pre-switch rules and attend to the post-switch dimension (Zelazo et al., 2003). In this case, it seems that 3-year-olds have too little inhibition to suppress a prepotent response pattern.

The persistent perseveration across these two conditions leaves one wondering whether *any* changes in the features of the cards can improve performance in this task. Results from a Total-Change version speak to this issue: when the features of both dimensions are changed, 3-year-olds can reliably switch to sorting by the other dimension (Zelazo et al., 2003; see Figure 1F). Thus, if there is nothing to inhibit and the post-switch features have not been negatively primed, children can switch rules. These data indicate that single cause accounts such as inhibition or negative-priming at the level of specific features alone are not sufficient to fully capture the underlying processes giving rise to perseveration.

The Role of Working Memory

The DCCS does not place high demands on working memory capacity since only two rules are relevant for each game and these rules are repeated throughout the pre- and post-switch phases. Nevertheless, evidence shows that the strength of representations that are the basis for the different sets of rules critically influences performance. For example, 3-year-olds can switch rules if the representations utilized for the post-switch phase are stronger than those utilized for the pre-switch phase. Yerys and Munakata (2006) demonstrated this by manipulating the name used for the pre- and post-switch sorting games. Specifically, 3-year-olds' post-switch performance is improved if the pre-switch game is simply called a "sorting" game and the post-switch game is given a standard informative name (such as the "shape" or "color" game). This effect is also seen if the manipulation occurs at the level of specific stimulus features. For example, 3-year-olds' post-switch performance is improved if novel shapes or colors with novel labels are used during the pre-switch game while familiar features and labels are used for the post-switch game (Yerys & Munakta, 2006). In either case, it appears that an informative label can be maintained in working memory during the post-switch phase which can out-compete the less-familiar or non-informative representation used during the pre-switch phase.

The Role of Task Switching

Various manipulations to the transition between the pre- and post-switch phases have been shown to facilitate correct rule-switching. Specifically, if the post-switch rules are given while the target cards are removed or if the concepts of shape-rules and color-rules are explained in detail before the child sorts, 3-year-olds have less difficulty switching rules (Mack, 2007). Further, if children are instructed to play a "silly" version of the pre-switch game and to match the test cards to the opposite of the pre-switch features during the post-switch phase (e.g., matching red to blue and blue to red), 3-year-olds are able to switch rules (Kloo, Perner, Kerschhuber, Dabernig, & Aichhorn, 2008; however, see also Brooks, Hanauer, Padowska, & Rosman, 2003, who show children are worse with bi-dimensional stimuli than with uni-dimensional stimuli in this "silly" version of the task). This highlights that children's representation of the task-switch is critical to perseveration or success in the DCCS.

The Role of Feedback and Demonstration Cues

Three-year-olds are able to correctly switch rules if they are given sufficient demonstration cues or feedback. Specifically, if children receive direct feedback on their performance (Bohlman & Fenson, 2005), if children see the post-switch rules demonstrated (Towse, Redbond, Houston-Price, & Cook, 2000), or if children are told to wait and think about the rules before they sort a given card in the post-switch (Deák, Ray, & Pick, 2004), then their post-switch performance improves. Thus, even within the standard task structure, children are not completely rigid in their perseveration but can successfully switch given enough instruction.

The Role of Conflict

Children's ability to switch rules in the DCCS task is not simply based on the consistency of the features on the cards between the pre- and post-switch phases—*what* children sort also matters. For example, conflict between the dimensions during the pre-switch is necessary for perseveration. Zelazo et al. (2003) and Müller et al. (2006) showed that 3-year-olds no longer perseverate in the Standard or Negative Priming versions if the test cards match the target cards along both dimensions during the initial sorting phase (e.g., sorting red stars to red stars and blue circles to blue circles; see the no-conflict versions in Figure 1D,E). Further, if conflict is decreased by only using one feature within the irrelevant dimension during both the pre- and post-switch phases (see Relational Complexity version in Figure 1G) children have less difficulty switching rules (Halford, Bunch, & McCredden, 2007).

Visual conflict can be further eliminated by using pictures of cartoon characters in lieu of target cards (the characters being characterized as "wanting" one feature or another; Perner & Lang, 2002) or by completely removing target cards and having children sort to empty trays (Towse et al., 2000). Under these circumstances, 3-year-olds have little trouble switching rules. The results with target cards absent are particularly interesting given the supposedly heightened demands on rule-representation in the absence of visual cues.

The Role of Feature Binding

Switching rules can also be facilitated if the "objecthood" of the images on the cards is eliminated by separating the features on the cards (e.g., an outline of a star next to a patch of blue; see Figure 1H; Diamond, Carlson, & Beck, 2005; Kloo & Perner, 2005; Zelazo et al., 2003). Further, 3-year-olds can switch rules if the dimensions are separated into four sorting locations with univalent target cards (e.g., a black outline of a star or circle and patches of red or blue) so that different pairs of trays are used for the color and shape rules (all four trays are displayed throughout the pre- and post-switch; Rennie, Bull, & Diamond, 2004). These versions highlight that children's difficulty is not just a function of the "rules" in the task, but is also influenced by the nature of the objects to which children apply the rules. Specifically, children benefit from being able to apply the shape and color rules to different objects. This suggests that processes of object representation or selective attention are central aspects of children's rule-use.

Review of Neuroimaging Studies

Research on the DCCS task has focused on early childhood, typically the age range from 3 to 5 years. This is a difficult time period to collect neuroimaging data because the gold standard of neuroimaging methods— fMRI—is not suitable for 3-year-olds. Consequently, researchers have turned to a new neuroimaging method—fNIRS—to study the early development of EF. In the one study of this type, Moriguchi and Hiraki (2009) used fNIRS to examine changes in frontal cortex activation as young children engaged in the standard DCCS task. They found increases in inferior prefrontal cortex activity between 3 and 5 years associated with rule-shifting in the DCCS. In particular, 3- and 5-year-olds that were able to switch rules also showed significantly stronger frontal activation compared to 3-year-olds who perseverated. This suggests that changes in the engagement of the frontal cortex support the early emergence of flexible rule-use.

Another way to examine the neural processes that underlie performance in the DCCS task is to use fMRI with older children and adults. Morton et al.

(2009) used fMRI to explore differences in neural activation between 11- to 13-year-olds and adults when shifting dimensional attention in the DCCS task. This study showed that activation in superior parietal cortex, dorsolateral PFC, pre-supplementary motor area, inferior frontal junction, and fusiform gyrus was associated with shifting rules in the DCCS. Further, between adolescence and adulthood, there are increases in activation in superior parietal cortex, superior frontal sulcus, and fusiform gyrus. In addition to this study, Nagahama et al. (2001) used fMRI with adults and compared dimensional shifts of attention with simple response reversals for the features (akin to the "silly" version reviewed above; Kloo et al., 2008). Shifting rules, regardless of whether attention was also being shifted, activated inferior frontal sulcus. However, middle frontal gyrus was selectively activated when shifts of attention were required.

Summary of Behavioral and Neural Studies

The rich behavioral literature on the DCCS provides robust constraints for the development of a theory of EF. Children fail to switch rules in very specific ways, showing robust perseveration across many variants of the task. Interestingly, however, 3-year-olds can switch under particular circumstances when the demands on inhibition, WM, or task switching are decreased. Thus, an integrative theory of the early development of EF must explain why young children perseverate in some circumstances, why they succeed in others, and what changes over development to create robust rule-switching across tasks.

The neuroimaging literature on the DCCS task has revealed several networks that are selectively activated in this task and are associated with different aspects of EF. Moriguchi and Hiraki's (2009) study showed increases in frontal activation when 3- and 5-year-olds switch rules. This is consistent with data showing developmental changes in the functional connectivity of frontal and posterior areas (Dosenbach et al., 2007; Fair et al., 2007). fMRI data with adults, however, has revealed a more detailed network of cortical areas related to different aspects of rule-switching that emerges through childhood and adolescence. Although the picture regarding the neural basis of EF and rule-switching is incomplete, there are sufficient data to take seriously the bridge between brain and behavior. In the next section, we discuss how current theories account for this pattern of behavioral and neural data.

Current Theories of the Development of Executive Function

Our review of the empirical literature on the DCCS task reveals a complicated pattern of results where *everything seemingly matters*. The DCCS, then, presents a formidable theoretical challenge. Are existing theories up to this challenge? Theories that address the development of executive function within the context of the DCCS task run the gamut from an information processing theory framed around hierarchical rule representation (Zelazo et al., 2003), to conceptual accounts of the task framed around attentional inertia (Kirkham, Cruess, & Diamond, 2003) or redescription (Kloo & Perner, 2005), to a formal connectionist model framed around active versus latent representations (Morton & Munakata, 2002). Below, we discuss the extant accounts in turn, building from abstract conceptual accounts at one end of the theoretical spectrum, to formally implemented models at the other end of the spectrum.

Cognitive Complexity and Control Theory

The most comprehensive account of children's performance in the DCCS task to date is the Cognitive Complexity and Control theory (CCC; Zelazo, 2004; Zelazo et al., 2003). CCC is an information-processing theory that conceptualizes children's behavior and development around hierarchical rule-representation. This theory contends that for children to be successful in the post-switch phase of the DCCS, they need to be able to consciously reflect on the two sets of rules and construct a representation of a rule structure that can integrate the rules for the different featural dimensions. This enables them to select the appropriate rules given the game being played.

To construct a set of rules for the color or shape game, specific feature values (i.e., *antecedent conditions*) are connected to a location where the feature is to be sorted (i.e., *consequences*). This rule representation takes the form of an if-then production rule that reads, "if red, then place the card here, but if blue, then place the card there." Sets of antecedent conditions and consequences are linked at the next higher level in the hierarchy in a relationship between the dimensions of the rules (i.e., *setting conditions*) that specify when the different sets of rules should be used (see Figure 2). Integrating this representation with the representation of the individual rule sets also takes the form of an if-then statement reading, for example, "if color game and if red, then sort here, but if shape game and if circle, then sort there."

To engage a set of rules during the pre-switch phase, the child must make an active decision to use a particular set of rules given the conflict created by the test card matching both of the target cards in some way. The active nature of this decision was captured in a subsequent revision of CCC theory, CCC-r, which incorporated the dynamics of activation and inhibition of rule sets (Zelazo et al., 2003). Specifically, one set of rules is used in the pre-switch phase and gains a high level of activation, while the other rule set is inhibited and decreases in activation. Going into the post-switch phase, children must engage the second setting condition via a top-down process driven by

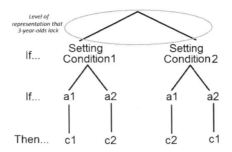

FIGURE 2.—The rule-hierarchy of the Cognitive Complexity and Control (CCC) theory (Zelazo et al., 2003). Setting conditions determine if shape or color rules are to be used. The *a*'s stand for *antecedent conditions*, which correspond to the different features of each dimension (*a1* goes with *a1* and *a2* with *a2* under each setting condition as the combination of features on the test cards). The *c*'s stand for *consequences*, which correspond to the different decisions to be made for each feature (i.e., where the card is to be placed).

reflection on the rule-structure. Without the representation of setting conditions in a second level of the rule hierarchy, children default to the more active set of rules that were initially used during the pre-switch. Thus, 3-year-olds are able to construct separate branches of antecedent conditions and consequences and are able to use these representations to sort cards during the pre-switch or answer questions about the post-switch rules. Nevertheless, they lack the ability to integrate both branches of rules under the setting conditions at a second level in the hierarchy. As the prefrontal cortex develops, this cortical area is able to represent increasingly complex rule-structures, allowing the child to construct a rule-hierarchy that allows for the top-down selection of the appropriate setting condition (see Bunge & Zelazo, 2006).

Using these concepts of rule-representation and activation, CCC-r theory can explain results of the Negative Priming and Partial-Change versions. In either situation, the rules that apply to the pre-switch dimension are more active during the post-switch phase either because the rules for the post-switch dimension were inhibited during the pre-switch (Negative Priming version; Figure 1B) or the rules for the pre-switch dimension have a high level of activation after being used in the pre-switch phase (Partial-Change version; Figure 1C). This imbalance of activation—even when one set of features changes—requires a rule-hierarchy for the top-down selection of the appropriate rules during the post-switch phase. Zelazo et al. (2003) further state that negative priming and the persistent activation of rule-sets depend on actively selecting a set of rules against a competing alternative. Thus, in the no-conflict Standard (Figure 1D) and No-Conflict Negative Priming versions (Figure 1E), children are able to use two un-integrated branches of rules

20

successively because the processes of inhibition and negative priming no longer have significant contributions to the activation of rules within the hierarchy. With the shape and color rules acquiring equal levels of activation, simply telling the child to use a different set of rules provides sufficient activation to use those rules during the post-switch phase.

By structuring the rule-hierarchy around the different dimensions of the visual features (i.e., the setting conditions), CCC/CCC-r theory is able to generate various predictions that have been empirically supported. For example, Zelazo et al. (2003) showed that 3-year-olds are unable to switch between single rules for features within different visual dimensions or setting conditions. Three-year-olds were asked to sort a single test card containing an image of a green car within the standard task-space structure containing two sorting locations with target cards. When playing the green game, the card was to be sorted by color, but if playing the car game the card was to be sorted by its shape. Even with these simpler branches containing a single rule under each setting condition, 3-year-olds perseverated on the rule they used first. Zelazo et al. (2003) further showed that 3-year-olds are able to use four rules at once (e.g., using four color rules) and switch between sets of rules if they are under the same setting condition (e.g., switching between two sets of color rules using red and blue, or green and yellow). Thus, the number of rules under different setting conditions does not necessarily matter. This indicates that children's difficulty does not stem from a limitation in memory capacity or from a general difficulty in switching rules. Rather, 3-year-olds only have trouble when the pairs of rules require attention to different visual dimensions and, thus, span separate branches of the rule-hierarchy.

Although CCC/CCC-r theory generalizes to a broad range of effects, it has critical limitations as well. For example, CCC/CCC-r theory does not specify how children learn to construct complex rule-hierarchies over development. Although this theory proposes that rule-use is grounded in emergence from more basic process, the theory is focused on the conscious decisions made by the child and does not attempt to explain the real-time process of forming and engaging rules. In this sense, although CCC/CCC-r uses neural concepts, it is not well-positioned to integrate brain and behavior. Rather, ties to neural dynamics and development have remained largely at the descriptive level (Bunge & Zelazo, 2006). Further, CCC/CCC-r falls short of accounting for different aspects of EF because it explains performance in the DCCS using a specialized rule-switching system. Finally, there are empirical data that highlight a fundamental limitation of an abstract rule representation framework. Specifically, 3-year-olds can more easily switch to attentionally salient, distinctive features than less salient, perceptually similar features (Fisher, 2011; Honomichl & Chen, 2011). In this case, the rule-hierarchy is the same, but performance is influenced by the attentional salience of the features involved in the different tasks. Thus, CCC/CCC-r theory does not

21

specify how the salience or similarity of features, or attentional manipulations in general, influences reflection on the rule-structure, the representation of rule pairs, or the activation of rule pairs.

Other Conceptual Accounts

An alternative account, the Attentional Inertia hypothesis (Kirkham et al., 2003), moves away from the concept of rule-representation and instead attributes children's perseveration to inflexible attention. In particular, when using a particular set of rules, children must selectively attend to a visual dimension of the stimulus. Children perseverate because attention becomes stuck on the featural dimension to which it is initially applied. Shifting attention, then, requires the active inhibition or suppression of the current deployment of attention. By inhibiting and disengaging, attention becomes free to shift to a different dimension of the stimuli. With poorly developed inhibitory control, the child is unable to disengage, and is thus unable to refocus her attention on the new dimension to use the post-switch rules.

To support their account, Kirkham et al. (2003) showed that boosting attention to the post-switch features by prompting children to relabel the test cards during the post-switch by the relevant dimension significantly improved children's ability to switch rules (however, see also Müller, Zelazo, Lurye, & Liebermann, 2008, for a failure to replicate these results in a series of experiments). Kirkham et al. (2003) further showed that sorting cards face-up impaired 5-year-olds' ability to switch rules. They suggest that this manipulation provided an even stronger pull on attention to the pre-switch dimension, making attention even more inflexible. Diamond and Kirkham (2005) also found evidence for attentional inertia with adults in a timed version of the DCCS. Adults showed significantly slower reaction times on the trials immediately following a switch in rules, suggesting that it even takes adults extra time to shift their attention to another featural dimension.

Another alternative account put forth by Kloo et al. (2008) and Kloo and Perner (2005)—the redescription hypothesis—frames children's difficulty in the DCCS around an inability to redescribe objects. They suggest that children use a more general matching strategy along dimensions (e.g., match by color) than a hierarchy of rules. For this strategy to work, however, children need to engage descriptions of the objects along the correct dimension. Children fail to switch in this case, because they have difficulty redescribing the test cards by the new dimension. If children can apply a new label to a different object, they should have little trouble switching rules. This appears to be the case: 3-year-olds succeed with separated dimensions where they can describe a patch of color as red and the outline of the shape as a star (Perner & Lang, 2002; Zelazo et al., 2003). Further, when the post-switch is introduced as a "silly" version of the first game and children are instructed to match the pre-switch features to the opposite target cards, children do not need to redescribe the test cards by the new dimension and they typically succeed. What develops to allow correct rule-switching, according to this view, is "a conceptual understanding that things can be described differently under different perspectives" (Kloo et al., 2008, p. 132).

The attentional inertia and redescription hypotheses offer different ways of describing children's behavior in the DCCS task. The attentional inertia hypothesis lacks a clear definition of attention, which is problematic given the complexity of this cognitive construct (for a review, see Luck & Vecera, 2002). Specifically, it is unclear what type of attention is involved, what mechanisms are involved in changes in attention, or how the influence of inhibitory control on attention changes over development. Similarly, the redescription hypothesis does not offer an account of what processes underlie children's ability to apply flexible descriptions or what mechanisms produce changes in children's concepts that support flexible descriptions. Thus, it is difficult to determine exactly how well these accounts capture behavior, how they generalize beyond the DCCS task, and what develops to enable flexible behavior.

Connectionist Model

Morton and Munakata (2002) took an important step toward formalizing the neural and developmental mechanisms underlying the DCCS by implementing this task in a connectionist model (see Figure 3). In the model, relevant dimensions are represented within a set of PFC nodes. These nodes reflect the dimensionality of the stimulus, representing either shape or color as the relevant dimension. When the model *actively* represents either the shape or color "rules" in the PFC nodes, the feed-forward connections between the hidden units and output units for the relevant features are strengthened. As inputs are processed and "sorted" according to the pre-switch dimension, *latent* connections are established through a Hebbian process between the hidden layer and output nodes. Importantly, only the

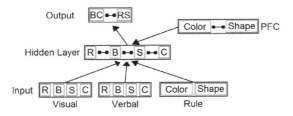

FIGURE 3.—The parallel distributed processing (PDP) model proposed by Morton and Munakata (2002). Visual, verbal, and rule inputs are fed through a hidden layer and a prefrontal cortex (PFC) layer (which also feeds into the hidden layer and modifies the strength of the connections between the hidden layer and the output layer). Decisions are made in the output layer for which target card the test card should be matched.

23

features that are used for sorting undergo Hebbian learning. This creates a bias in the system toward making decisions based on that dimension. For the model to overcome these latent connections and correctly sort by the post-switch rules, the PFC nodes need to have a relatively strong active representation of the current rules to shift the balance of activation between hidden layer and output layer toward making decisions based on the post-switch dimension. As the PFC develops (i.e., as the strength of recurrent activation in the model's PFC nodes is increased), the model is able to actively represent the relevant rules, exerting a stronger influence on the decision-making process and facilitating flexible rule-use.

This model has generated various predictions about children's rule-use in the DCCS task. For example, Morton and Munakata (2002) gave their model practice with unidimensional post-switch inputs before the start of the post-switch phase. This increased the strength of latent traces for the post-switch features and improved the performance of the model. Brace et al. (2006) tested this prediction by administering a training phase between the pre- and post-switch phases. The training phase consisted of a set of cards that started with univalent stimuli for the post-switch features. Throughout the training phase, the pre-switch features were gradually "morphed" into the image on the cards until they contained fully bivalent stimuli when the child started the post-switch phase. This training phase significantly improved 3-year-olds' post-switch performance over that of children who had a training phase with irrelevant features or dimensions.

In a second test of the model, Jordan and Morton (2008) explored the role that environmental support can have in promoting the active representations of new rules. They showed that children are better able to switch rules with the use of congruent flankers. For instance, if color was the relevant post-switch dimension, patches of color would flank the test-card image. With this extra environment support, children can activate the relevant task rules more strongly and correctly switch rules. Finally, the studies examining the influence of dimensional labels or novel features reviewed above (Yerys & Munakata, 2006) were designed to probe the active/latent memory distinction in the model. Specifically, when the pre-switch game is simply called a "sorting" game, or when unfamiliar features are used for the pre-switch game, weaker latent memories are established that pose less competition with the active memories during the post-switch phase.

The account offered by Morton and Munakata (2002) has many strengths. It uses a neurally plausible implementation of rule-use and has generated multiple empirical predictions that have been successfully tested. Nonetheless, this theory does not achieve as much coverage of the DCCS literature as CCC/CCC-r theory. In particular, the model has not been generalized to account for other versions of the task to explain, for example, why children still perseverate in the NP version or are able to switch in versions where there is no conflict during the pre-switch phase. Indeed, there are no dimensions per se in the model; there are only associations between the PFC and hidden units representing the particular features of the task. Thus, it is unclear how the model would capture the introduction of new features at different phases of sorting. Interestingly, the model has not been used to quantitatively capture children's performance or changes over development, although Morton and Munakata (2002) have demonstrated that correct switching increases as the recurrent connections for the PFC nodes are strengthened.

Summary of theories

The theoretical perspectives reviewed here offer differing views of what a "rule" is and how the ability to use rules changes over development. CCC/CCC-r theory has been used to conceptually integrate an extensive portion of the literature but lacks specification of several key processes and an ability to interface with neural data. The connectionist model put forth by Morton and Munakata (2002), at the other extreme, uses formal neural concepts but has not been used to explain a broad array of findings in the literature.

Our primary aim in developing the DNF model described below is to achieve extensive theoretical coverage of young children's performance in the DCCS task early in development while adhering to, and anchoring our concepts in, formalized neural principles. This brain-behavior focus is inspired by data showing not only the complexity of explaining cognitive flexibility at the neural level, but also the promise that this level of explanation might offer new ways to test and constrain developmental theories of EF. In the present work, we take a first step toward this brain-behavior link, showing that DFT sheds light on EF by integrating different functional aspects of control within a single model and providing insight into the neural processes associated with different aspects of rule-use and EF. In this way, the model offers useful clarity about the link between cognitive concepts and their neural instantiation.

III. DYNAMIC FIELD THEORY

Dynamic Field Theory (DFT) grew out of the principles and concepts of dynamical systems theory initially explored in the "motor approach" pioneered by Gregor Schöner, Esther Thelen, Scott Kelso, Michael Turvey, and others (e.g., Kelso, Scholz, & Schöner, 1988; Schöner & Kelso, 1988; Thelen & Smith, 1994; Turvey & Shaw, 1995). The goal was to develop a formal, neurally grounded theory that could bring the concepts of dynamical systems theory to bear on issues in cognition and cognitive development. DFT was initially applied to issues closely aligned with the cognitive aspects of motor systems such as motor planning for arm and eye movements (Erlhagen & Schöner, 2002; Kopecz & Schöner, 1995). Subsequent work extended DFT, capturing a wide array of phenomena in the area of spatial cognition, from spatial category biases to changes in the metric precision of spatial working memory from childhood to adulthood (Schutte, Spencer, & Schöner, 2003; Simmering, Schutte, & Spencer, 2008). This theoretical framework has been used to capture how objects are neurally represented in a way that links features to a spatial frame of reference (Johnson, Spencer, & Schöner, 2008; Schneegans, Lins, & Spencer, in press; Spencer, Schneegans, & Schöner, in press), how object recognition can emerge from associating features with labels (Faubel & Schöner, 2008), and how young children learn words in a social context using a common spatial frame to bind words and objects together (Samuelson, Smith, Perry, & Spencer, 2011).

Importantly, the model we present here was not derived solely as a model of rule-use; rather, it is an extension of an object WM model (Johnson et al., 2008; Spencer, Austin et al., 2012; see also Samuelson et al., 2011) to which we add an autonomous dimensional attention system. Rule-use, then, emerges in the neural interaction between dimensional attention nodes (a "shape" or "color" node) and an object WM system that localizes features in space and makes decisions about where objects should be placed. We show how this interactive system captures young children's performance in the DCCS task. We then use the DNF model to probe whether specific developmental changes in the dimensional attention system are sufficient to capture the emergence of flexible rule-use in the DCCS task between 3 and 5 years.

In the following sections, we describe the DNF model. It is important to note that when we refer to terms such as neural activation, cortical fields, and excitatory/inhibitory neural interactions, we are referring to the *simulated* neural dynamics of the model. Although we do not capture actual neural measurements from children in the present study, DFT has a long history of interfacing directly with neural data (see Bastian et al., 1998, 2003; Buss, Wifall, Hazeltine, & Spencer, 2014; Erlhagen et al., 1999; Jancke et al., 1999; Markounikau et al., 2010; McDowell et al., 2002; Spencer et al., 2012). As we discuss below, these previous reports show that the neural concepts we use when describing the DNF framework are more than just neural jargon: these are well-grounded concepts that can be mapped to neural measures commonly used in the literature (e.g., multi-unit recording, voltage-sensitive dye imaging, and ERPs).

We begin with an overview of several central concepts in DFT, including a discussion of neural population dynamics within multilayered cortical fields, interactions between different cortical fields, as well as the variant of Hebbian learning we use to capture changes in neural dynamics over a trial-to-trial timescale (see, Faubel & Schöner, 2008; Lipinski, Spencer, & Samuelson, 2010; Samuelson et al., 2011; Simmering et al., 2008). Next, we describe the object WM model (Johnson et al., 2008; Spencer et al., in press; see also, Samuelson et al., 2011). This is followed by an overview of the dimensional attention system that we couple to this model, as well as a discussion of the developmental hypotheses explored in the present study. We then step through how the DNF model sorts cards in a rule-like fashion in the DCCS task, perseverating early in development and switching rules later in development. Finally, we conclude with a discussion of how the DNF model achieves the different functional aspects of cognitive control discussed in Chapter I.

Basic Concepts of DFT

DFT simulates thinking in the form of neural population dynamics, that is, patterns of neural activity within cortical fields consisting of simulated neurons "tuned" to continuous metric dimensions (e.g., space, color, orientation; for related ideas, see, e.g., Georgopolous, Schwartz, & Kettner, 1986). These fields are organized so that neighboring locations in a field have similar receptive fields—they respond maximally to similar feature values. Moreover, neighboring neurons share lateral excitatory interactions, such that the activity of one neuron can boost the activity of its neighbors. By contrast, neurons with very different receptive fields share inhibitory interactions, such that the activity of a local group of neurons can inhibit the activity of neurons tuned to different feature values (for discussion, see Spencer, Austin, & Schutte, 2012). When inputs to such a field are strong enough to reach an activation threshold (an activation level of 0), these inputs combine with lateral interactions among neurons (local excitation, surround

27

inhibition) to form "peaks" of activation that stably represent a particular feature value. These peaks represent a type of neural decision that a particular feature value is, for instance, present in the world. Moreover, if neural interactions are strong enough, peaks can remain stably activated through time—even in the absence of sensory stimulation. In this sense, peaks can capture key properties of "working" or "active" memory (Compte, Brunel, Goldman-Rakic, & Wang, 2000; Edin et al., 2007, 2009; Johnson, Spencer, & Schöner, 2009).

In the present report, we use two-layered neural fields composed of an excitatory layer of neurons (which we call a working memory [WM] field) coupled to a layer of inhibitory interneurons (Inhib field). When activation reaches an activation threshold (>0), the WM field becomes self-excitatory—that is, activated neurons share excitation with close neighbors. Also, the activated neurons pass excitation to the Inhib field. Once these inhibitory interneurons are activated at above-threshold levels (>0), they pass broad inhibition back into WM. This dynamic back-and-forth among layers creates the local excitatory and laterally inhibitory interactions needed to form localized peaks within the field (see the Appendix for a more detailed discussion and the two-layered neural field equations).

Our DNF models also use a variant of Hebbian learning that allows neural populations to learn as they acquire a history in the task (see, e.g., Lipinski, Simmering, Johnson, & Spencer, 2010; Lipinski et al., 2010; see Perone, Simmering, & Spencer, 2011; see Clearfield, Dineva, Smith, Diedrich, & Thelen, 2009). These Hebbian memories vary in strength from 0 to 1, much like a "weight" or synaptic connection in a connectionist model. As Hebbian memories increase in strength, the affected neurons acquire a resting level closer to the activation threshold of 0 (i.e., the resting level becomes less negative). Thus, Hebbian memories enable specific neural sites in the field to become activated more quickly on subsequent trials. This results in a priming effect, facilitating the response of a local population of neurons to a familiar stimulus.

A central question with any neural network framework is how the concepts of the theory are anchored to the neural reality of the brain. On this front, DFT is well-grounded. The layered architecture we use was initially developed to capture neural activation patterns within visual cortex (Amari, 1977, 1980; Amari & Arbib, 1977; see also, Compte et al., 2000; Wilson & Cowan, 1972). Our coworkers have demonstrated that the population dynamics within neural fields can be directly derived from multi-unit neurophysiology using the Distribution of Population Activation approach (Bastian et al., 1998, 2003; Erlhagen et al., 1999; Jancke et al., 1999). A related approach has also been used with voltage-sensitive dye imaging (VSDI; see Markounikau et al., 2010). These approaches enable researchers to directly test DNF models using neurophysiological measures in nonhuman animals.

Other efforts have shown that DNF models can be tested with humans using event-related potentials (see Spencer, Barich et al., 2012). For instance, McDowell et al. (2002) examined the prediction of a DNF model of motor planning that movement direction and response probability should be interdependent. They tested this by measuring both reaction times and the amplitude of the P300 event-related potential (a positive going event-related potential that peaks at 300 ms post stimulus onset). Both types of measures showed the predicted interactions. In summary, then, the differential equations that we use in the present report capture real, observable aspects of activation dynamics within populations of cortical neurons.

A DNF Model of Object WM

The model we propose here is based, in part, on a model of object working memory shown in Figure 4 (see Appendix for equations). At the top of this figure, we show a picture of the brain, with several highlighted cortical regions whose function is captured by aspects of the model. Below this is a simulation of the model at different points in time as it "binds" object features present in the visual display.

The architecture of the object WM model was inspired by the properties of the primate visual system, which has distinct processing pathways for visual information (Haxby et al., 1991; Ungerleider & Mishkin, 1982): a dorsal ("where") pathway that is primarily concerned with encoding the spatial locations of objects (e.g., Andersen, 1995) and a ventral ("what") pathway that is composed of cortical fields that encode different object features such as color or orientation in distinct neural populations (e.g., Desimone & Gross, 1979; Xiao, Wang, & Fellman, 2003). This creates a "binding" problem in vision (Treisman, 1996; Treisman & Gelade, 1980): given that different populations of neurons are tuned to different feature dimensions in the ventral pathway, how does the brain know which features go with which other features to quickly form a novel, integrated object representation?

Figure 4 shows a concrete example of this challenge: when shown the blue square and the yellow diamond in the display in Figure 4A, how does the brain know that the blue hue (represented by the dark gray shading of the object in the Display panel) should be linked to the square shape given that these neural representations "live" in different parts of the brain? Concretely, how does the brain know that the "blue" neurons in the fusiform area (see light gray circle on brain image; Simmons et al., 2007) should be coupled to the "square" neurons in the lateral occipital complex (see medium gray circle on brain image; Drucker & Aguirre, 2009; Kourtzi, Erb, Grodd, & Bülthoff, 2003)? One candidate solution to this problem is to capitalize on the bimodal nature of neural populations in the ventral stream. In particular, ventral stream neurons are sensitive to visual features but are also coarsely receptive to

29

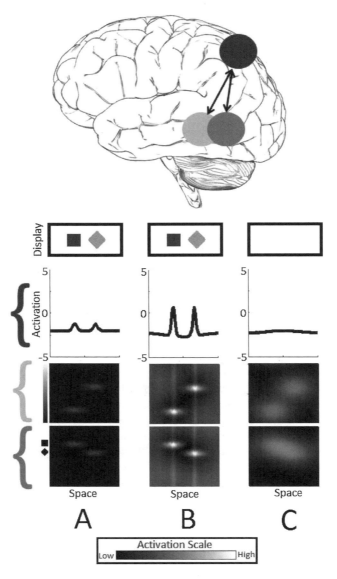

FIGURE 4.—Working memory (WM) fields for the feature binding model. Panel A depicts the model just after the inputs have been turned on. Panel B shows the WM fields after the inputs have reached threshold. Within fields, the neural interactions have been engaged to form a peak. Between fields, spatial activation is being shared (visible in the feature WM fields as the vertical ridge of activation) to anchor features together in the representation of an object with a particular shape and color. In Panel C the WM fields are shown after the inputs have turned off and excitation has relaxed to resting level. The contribution from Hebbian memory is now visible. The left panel shows the putative mapping of the different fields to cortical locations.

spatial information (see Aggelopoulos & Rolls, 2005; DiCarlo & Maunsell, 2003; Op De Beek & Vogels, 2000; for a review, see Kravitz, Vinson, & Baker, 2008). Thus, it might be possible to anchor the featural representations in both cortical areas to a precise representation of spatial locations in, for instance, parietal cortex (see dark gray circle on brain image; Andersen, 1995; for a review, see Silver & Kastner, 2009). This is the solution that the DNF model implements.

The sequence of simulations in Figure 4 illustrates how the DNF model "binds" visual features together. The top row of this figure shows the display of inputs that is presented to the model at three different time-points: at the onset of the display (A), after the objects have been consolidated or "bound" in working memory (B), and after the display has been turned off and the trial has ended (C). The next row shows a one-dimensional spatial field that captures aspects of neural processing in the parietal cortex (see dark gray circle on brain image). This field consists of a layer of neurons with receptive fields sensitive to variations in the horizontal positions of objects in the display. Neurons that "prefer" leftward locations in the display are on the left side of the spatial field, while neurons that "prefer" rightward locations in the display are on the right side of the spatial field. The x-axis in this figure shows the activation of each neuron in the field. For instance, in panel A, the two bumps of activation show the initial response of spatially tuned neurons to the presentation of an item to the left of center (the square) and a second item to the right of center (a diamond).

Below the spatial field in Figure 4A is a two-dimensional color-space field (which we will refer to as the "color" field). This layer of neurons has receptive fields sensitive to the combination of spatial position and color (hue), like neural populations in the fusiform area (light gray circle on brain image; see Simmons et al., 2007). Considered together, the entire two-dimensional field of neurons can represent any collection of colors at any location in the task space. The spatial tuning of the neurons is again shown along the x-axis, while the y-axis now displays the color tuning of the neurons (represented by the gray scale to the left of the field, which shows the mapping of the RGB color spectrum to the y-axis). The level of activation of neurons in the color field is depicted by the gray shading, with higher levels of activation indicated by lighter shading (see activation scale at bottom). As can be seen in the color field in Figure 4A, there is an activation bump (light gray oval) in the lower left region of the field that reflects the initial encoding of the blue (dark gray) square to the left, and a second bump of activation in the upper right region of the field that reflects the initial encoding of the yellow (light gray) diamond to the right.

Finally, the bottom panels in Figure 4 show the activation within a two-dimensional shape-space field (called the "shape" field). Here, these neurons have receptive fields that are sensitive to spatial position and shape information as in the lateral occipital complex (dark gray circle on brain image; see, e.g., Kourtzi et al., 2003). Like the color field, the x-axis shows the spatial tuning of the neurons while the y-axis shows the tuning along an abstract shape-similarity dimension. As before, the level of activation for these neurons is depicted by the gray shading (see activation scale at bottom). Thus, the activation bump in the upper left region of the field (light gray oval) reflects the initial encoding of the square on the left, and the activation bump to the lower right reflects the initial encoding of the diamond on the right.[1]

In Figure 4A, all of the activation profiles are sub-threshold (i.e., activation < 0) because the objects were just presented in the display. Thus, strong neural interactions have not yet become engaged, and the model has not formed robust WM representations of the objects. Critically, the coarse spatial encoding properties of the feature-space fields produces overlap along the spatial dimension for the feature inputs. Left alone, these bimodal cortical fields would have difficulty binding the correct colors to the correct shapes (for a demonstration of this difficulty, see Johnson et al., 2008).

Figure 4B shows the model resolving this ambiguity through spatial coupling. Since all of the WM fields share a common spatial dimension, activation is coupled along this dimension (see bi-directional arrows between dorsal and ventral cortical areas in the brain image). As activation rises, spatial information is passed back and forth among the WM fields. Because the spatial field has precise spatial information, this helps resolve any spatial conflict in the feature-space fields. This is shown in Figure 4B, which shows the fields after peaks have emerged. As can be seen, the model correctly binds "blue" and "square" on the left and "yellow" and "diamond" on the right. In particular, there are robust peaks to the left and right of the spatial field (second panel), at the blue hue value to the left and yellow hue value to the right in the color field (third panel), and at the square shape to the left and diamond shape to the right in the shape field (bottom panel). *Note that the shared spatial excitation can be seen in the vertical ridges within the feature-space fields.* Although activation is passing back-and-forth at the left and right spatial positions, this does not lead to explosive excitation at every sight along these ridges; rather, the lateral or surround inhibition associated with each peak in the feature-space fields keep excitation locally contained around the consolidated object feature values. This spatial coupling and associated feature binding will play a critical role in the simulations of the DCCS that we discuss below.

Figure 4C shows the fields after the inputs have been turned off and the "trial" is over. This reveals the contribution from the Hebbian process that operates in the model: there is now slightly elevated activation corresponding to the blue square that was on the left and the yellow diamond that was on the right. As can be seen, these memories are very coarse, elevating broad regions around sites associated with the WM peaks in Figure 4B. What is the consequence of the broad memory traces? When these, or similar objects, are presented again, peaks will build more readily at these particular feature-space conjunctions given the slightly elevated activation levels.

To summarize, in the DNF model, neural populations that code for different object features are bound together by a common spatial dimension anchored to the precise spatial representations found in the parietal cortex. Note that this solution to the binding problem shares elements with Feature Integration Theory proposed by Treisman and Gelade (1980). Further, as the model builds integrated WM representations across the different cortical fields, a Hebbian learning process operates to bring the activated sites closer to their activation threshold. This creates a type of priming effect when these objects are re-presented, causing neurons in the fields to become activated more quickly on subsequent presentations.

Autonomous Dimensional Attention and the Development of Rule-Use

The model shown in Figure 4 is able to actively form working memories and Hebbian associations for object features in the task space, but how does it sort cards and behave in a rule-like fashion in the DCCS task? For this, we need to add an additional concept—dimensional attention. Figure 5 shows the complete model architecture, which adds a frontal dimensional attention system. The brain image in Figure 5A adds a black circle highlighting several frontal cortical regions implicated in executive function and the control of dimensional attention (see, e.g., Morton et al., 2009). This frontal system is reciprocally coupled to cortical fields in the ventral and dorsal pathways as indicated by the bi-directional arrows (see Crone, Wendelken, Donohue, van Leijenhorst, & Bunge, 2006; Dosenbach et al., 2007).[2]

The architecture of the dimensional attention system in the model is shown in Figure 5B. This architecture consists of two attentional nodes labeled "color" and "shape." The nodes have the same dynamics as neural fields: they are self-excitatory, mutually inhibitory, and can show robust, above-threshold activation when sufficiently stimulated. In this sense, then, the nodes can be viewed as localized neural populations in frontal cortex that can enter a robust "peak" state when the system is actively attending to a particular type of information, such as shape or color. These nodes also learn as they are repeatedly activated in a task. In particular, the frontal system uses the same type of Hebbian process described previously. Hebbian traces at the level of the frontal system boost the baseline level of activation in the relevant node that can effectively prime "color" or "shape" responding on subsequent trials.

The information that each node actively represents is reflected in the pattern of connectivity between the frontal nodes in Figure 5B and the object WM system shown in Figure 5C. As is shown in the figure, the "color" node has

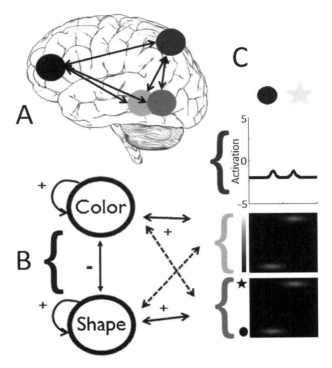

FIGURE 5.—The object working memory (WM) model, the dimensional attention architecture, and the putative mapping to cortex.

strong excitatory connections to the color field (solid bi-directional line) and weaker excitatory connections to the shape field (dashed bi-directional line). Consequently, when the "color" node goes into an active or "on" state, the color field receives a global activation boost. This makes it easier for peaks to form in the color field, which can bias the model to initially form peaks in the object WM system (Figure 5C) based on color information. Reversely, the "shape" node has strong excitatory connections to the shape field (solid bi-directional line) and weaker excitatory connections to the color field (dashed bi-directional line). Consequently, when the "shape" node goes into an active or "on" state, the shape field receives a global activation boost. This creates a bias in the model to initially form peaks in the object WM system (Figure 5C) based on shape information. This pattern of connectivity is akin to connection weights in a parallel distributed processing (PDP) network. We assume that the system begins with randomized weights that become selectively mapped as the "shape" dimensional neuron becomes associated with the shape field and the "color" dimensional neuron becomes associated

34

with the color field. Note that the pattern of connectivity in the model is fully reciprocal; thus, the growth of neural activity in the posterior neural fields (e.g., the shape and color fields) can also impact the activation of the frontal system.

The activation dynamics within our model are consistent with neurophysiological evidence (e.g., Egner & Hirsch, 2005; Lepsien & Nobre, 2007; Zanto, Rubens, Bollinger, & Gazzaley, 2010; Zanto, Rubens, Thangavel, & Gazzaley, 2011), which has demonstrated boosts in baseline activity for cortical areas processing task-relevant information under situations with high executive demands. For example, in a face/name Stroop task, boosts of baseline activity were observed in the fusiform face area on trials that required participants to categorize faces when conflicting names were presented.

In the present work, we probed whether specific changes in the connectivity pattern between the frontal and posterior cortical fields were sufficient to capture the emergence of rule-use over development in the DCCS task. In particular, we created a 3-year-old model that had poorly organized connectivity: activation of the "color" node, for instance, boosted the baseline level of activation in the color field, but also weakly boosted the shape field. By contrast, the 5-year-old model had well-organized connectivity: activation of the "color" node selectively boosted the color field and had little impact on the shape field (see Appendix for details). As we discuss below, these changes in connectivity were critical in capturing key aspects of young children's performance in the DCCS task. Conceptually, such changes are akin to changing the weight matrix in a PDP model over learning such that "shape" and "color" nodes become associated with a specific feature dimension.

In addition to refining the connectivity between the frontal and posterior neural systems in the model, we implemented a specific developmental hypothesis central to other work using DFT—the spatial precision hypothesis (Schutte & Spencer, 2009; Spencer et al., 2009). According to this hypothesis, excitatory and inhibitory neural interactions become stronger over development. Thus, the strength of self-excitation and lateral inhibition for the "shape" and "color" dimensional units was increased. This addresses the question of whether changes within the dimensional attention system are sufficient to capture the developmental pattern of behavior in the DCCS task.

Note that, although both developmental changes in the model—changes in the pattern of connectivity between frontal and posterior systems and changes in the strength of neural interactions in the dimensional attention system—were implemented "by hand," other work suggests that these changes could emerge via an autonomous learning mechanism. We highlight this direction in the General Discussion by describing work using DNFs. This work shows how patterns of connectivity between nodes and fields can be learned by standard forms of Hebbian learning as the system learns the correlation between, for instance, the use of the word "color" and the importance of task-relevant hue values in the task space (see Faubel & Schöner, 2008; Sandamirskaya & Schöner, 2010).

The DNF Model and the DCCS Task

Figure 6 shows the DNF model as it sorts cards in the DCCS task. The top panel shows the activation of the dimensional nodes across the pre-switch and post-switch phases for the young model (i.e., 3-year-olds). There are 12 periods where the dimensional nodes become more active (creating the box-car profile) corresponding to the six pre-switch and six post-switch trials. The middle panels show the object WM system at particular points during the task indicated by the time labels above each panel (which correspond to marked times on the top panel). The bottom panel shows the activation of the dimensional nodes for the older model (i.e., 5-year-olds). As is clear in this panel, the older model shows more robust activation of the dimensional attention system (i.e., greater activation values), with a clear separation in the activity of the "color" and "shape" nodes during the pre-switch and post-switch phases.

To understand how the model works in detail, it is important to dissect the neural interactions captured in the middle panel. Figure 6A shows the *target input* presented to the model. This input to each field in the object WM system reflects the presence of the target cards and trays used in the DCCS, for instance, the blue-circle on the left and the red-star on the right (see the display at the top of Figure 6A). In the spatial field, this input takes the form of subthreshold "bumps" of activation at the left and right locations. These serve to "pre-shape" or prime activation in the fields to build peaks at the locations of the trays, that is, to sort cards to these locations (for related ideas, see Erlhagen & Schöner, 2002). In the color field, there are two subthreshold hotspots of activation. These correspond to the blue item to the left and the red item to the right. There are also two subthreshold hotspots in the shape field. These correspond to the circle at the left location and the star at the right location. Thus, between the shape and color fields, there are inputs for a blue circle at the left tray and a red star at the right tray.

Figure 6B shows the object WM system just after an input for a red circle test card has been given. This *test input* is presented to the feature fields as horizontal ridges of activation for a feature across all spatial locations. This captures the nature of the task: the model, like children, must spatially localize the features presented on the test cards; that is, the model must decide to place the card to the left or right. Notice that there is spatial conflict between the two feature fields for the features presented on the test card in Figure 6B. The test input for the blue feature overlaps with the target input at the left location. The test input for the star feature, on the other hand,

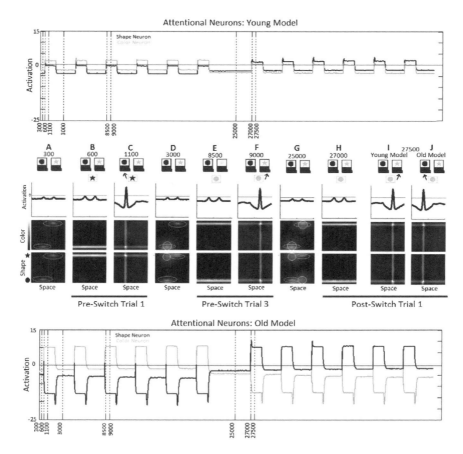

FIGURE 6.—The sequence of events as the model sorts cards in the Dimensional Change Card Sort (DCCS). For simplicity, only the spatial, color, and shape working memory (WM) fields are shown in each panel. The top panel depicts the activation of the dimensional attention nodes of the "young" model over the six pre- and six post-switch trials ("color" is plotted in light gray, "shape" is plotted in black). The middle panel shows the object WM system at particular timepoints of interest (see labels at top of Panels A–J). The bottom panel shows the activation of the dimensional attention nodes of the "older" model over the six pre- and post-switch trials. In this example, color is the relevant dimension for the pre-switch and shape is the relevant dimension for the post-switch. Panel A shows the inputs for the target cards and trays (highlighted by the gray ovals). Panel B shows the input for a blue star test card. Panel C shows the model sorting this card to the left. Panel D shows the formation of Hebbian traces from making that decision (highlighted by the white circle). Panels E and F show the inputs and decision being made for a red circle during the pre-switch phase. Panel G shows the WM fields of the model going into the post-switch phase after sorting during pre-switch phase. Gray ovals outline the target inputs, while white circles outline the Hebbian memories. Panel H shows the input for a red circle during the post-switch phase. Panel I shows the "young" model perseverating and sorting by color even though the "shape" node is now more strongly activated. Panel J shows the "old" model correctly switching and sorting by shape.

overlaps with the target input at the right location in the shape field. Thus, there is not enough information in these inputs alone to determine where the test input should be localized. The input for the blue feature will try to build a peak at the leftward location, while the input for the star feature will try to build a peak at the rightward location.

Critically, however, the model is "told" to play the color game at the beginning of the pre-switch phase. This is implemented as a sub-threshold input to the "color" node. This can be seen in the slight boost in activation for the "color" node (light gray line) in the top panel at timestep 300. As a test card is presented in panel B, the feature-space fields build-up excitation from the inputs. This sends activation to the dimensional nodes, boosting their activity (see the increase in activation in the top panel at timestep 600). The dimensional attention system, in turn, sends activation back to the feature-space fields, with a slight boost to the color field since the "color" node is more active. Figure 6C shows that this subtle bias in the activation of the "color" node is enough to tip the balance in the direction of a color-based decision: the model has formed a peak at the left location in the spatial field, binding the blue and star features to this location in the task space. Note that this spatial binding is reflected in the vertical ridges of subthreshold excitation at the leftward location in the feature-space fields as spatial information is passed back-and-forth among the object WM fields. Figure 6D shows the consequence of this sorting decision: there is a Hebbian memory in the color field that associates the blue feature and the left sorting location; similarly, there is a Hebbian memory in the shape field that associates the star feature and the left sorting location (see circled region of each field).

The same sequence of events play out as the model sorts the second type of test card highlighted in panels E–G. In Figure 6E, the model is shown a red circle to sort. This boosts the activity of the dimensional nodes (see top panel). The small bias to the "color" node is amplified, leading the model to sort the red circle based on its color. Consequently, the model forms a peak of activation to the right side of the color field, binds the circle feature to the right as well, and effectively sorts the red circle to the right (see Figure 6F).

Figure 6G shows the result of repeatedly sorting red circles to the right and blue stars to the left during the pre-switch phase: the model has robust Hebbian memories of where the test cards were sorted on the previous trials (see highlighted circles). Consider the consequences these memories will have as the model is now told to switch and play the shape game. In Figure 6G, the Hebbian traces are highlighted with white circles, while the target inputs are highlighted with white ovals. As can be seen in the figure, this results in *cooperation* within the color field—the Hebbian memories (circles) overlap with the target inputs (ovals). Consequently, activation is likely to build quickly at these primed locations. By contrast, there is *competition* within the shape field—the Hebbian memories (circles) associate the star shape with a leftward location and the circle shape with a rightward location, while the target inputs (ovals) indicate a circle on the left and a star on the right. Consequently, activation in this field will build slowly as multiple locations within the field compete through lateral inhibition.[3] Considered together, then, the pre-switch dimension (color) is primed and has a competitive advantage going into the post-switch phase.

What happens when the model transitions to the post-switch phase? As can be seen in the top panel at timestep 25,000, the post-switch phase begins with a boost to the "shape" node as the model is told to play the shape game. The "shape" node is given the same strength of input as the "color" node during the pre-switch phase; thus, the shape node (solid line) is now more strongly activated than the color node (gray line). Note, however, that the difference in the activation strengths of the two nodes is quite small—smaller, in fact, than at the start of the pre-switch phase (see timestep 300). This reflects the influence of Hebbian learning in the dimensional attention system. Specifically, Hebbian traces built up for the "color" node during the pre-switch phase. As a result, the "color" node is primed going into the post-switch phase, leading to a weaker differential in the activation of the two nodes.

At timestep 27,000, the model is given the first test card in the post-switch phase. In particular, Figure 6H shows a red circle test card that is presented to the object WM system. Figure 6I shows that the young model perseveratively sorts this red circle to the right—the model sorts by color and not shape. This occurs for two reasons: (1) there is only a small boost to the shape field from the dimensional attention system, and (2) there is cooperation in the color field and conflict in the shape field.

How is the model, like 5-year-olds, able to overcome these biases and switch rules? As discussed above, we made two changes to the model over development. First, the 5-year-old model has stronger interactions between the "shape" and "color" nodes—self-excitation and lateral inhibition are both stronger. This implements the spatial precision hypothesis probed in previous work using DFT (Schutte & Spencer, 2009; Spencer et al., 2009). Second, the connectivity pattern between the frontal and posterior systems is stronger and more selective. For example, the "shape" node now passes stronger excitation to and from the shape field and has relatively minimal interaction with the color field. Thus, the 5-year-old model has a more refined understanding of what "shape" means.

The bottom panel of Figure 6 shows how these developmental changes impact the activation of the dimensional attention system across the pre- and post-switch phases. Here, the relevant node for each phase achieves robust activation and strongly suppresses the irrelevant node. As a consequence, the 5-year-old model is now able to switch rules during the post-switch phase. This is shown in Figure 6J. In this figure, the 5-year-old model correctly sorts the red circle to the left—sorting by shape instead of color. The older model correctly sorts by shape because the "shape" node sends a strong boost of activity to the shape field and suppresses the activity of the "color" node (see timestep 27,500 in the bottom panel). With a stronger boost, the shape field can resolve the competition between the Hebbian memory and the test input, successfully sorting the red circle to the left.

To get a better feel for the differences in the neural dynamics between the young and the old model, Figure 7 zooms in on these neural dynamics during the critical moments when the model is making its initial sorting decision on the first post-switch trial. The top panel plots the activation of the dimensional attention system for the old (solid lines) and young (dashed lines) model. The middle and bottom panels show the object WM system for the young and old models, respectively, at critical time-points during the decision-making process. Because the spatial field is receiving the summed activation over space from the different feature-space fields, this field reflects the relative amount of conflict or cooperation in the feature-space fields as a decision is being made.

Figure 7A shows the fields before the first post-switch test card is presented. Note the cooperation within the color field and competition within the shape field for both models. In Figure 7B, the red circle test card is presented to the model. At the corresponding timestep (26,975), the dimensional attention system is just becoming engaged. In Figure 7C, the inputs from the test card have built close to threshold and spatial activation is being shared throughout the network. At this point in time in the spatial field, the left and right locations are roughly equally activated in both the young and old model. Consequently, it is not clear how the object WM system will sort the card at this point in time. Looking at the dimensional attention system, however, differences between the old and young models are evident (see timestep 27,000). Specifically, the "shape" and "color" neurons for the old model have achieved a much larger separation in activation relative to the young model. Thus, the old model is attending to, or boosting, the shape field more strongly and selectively than the young model. The consequences of this difference are starting to become evident in Figure 7D. The young model has stronger overall activation at the rightward location due to the cooperation in the color field, while the old model has stronger overall activation at the leftward location due to the input from the "shape" node to the shape field. Finally, in Figure 7E, both models have resolved the spatial conflict and made a sorting decision. The young model perseverated and sorted the red circle to the right, while the older model successfully switched and sorted the test card to the left.

Summary of the Model

We have presented a DNF model that consists of multiple, reciprocally coupled neural fields with featural and spatial properties common to neural

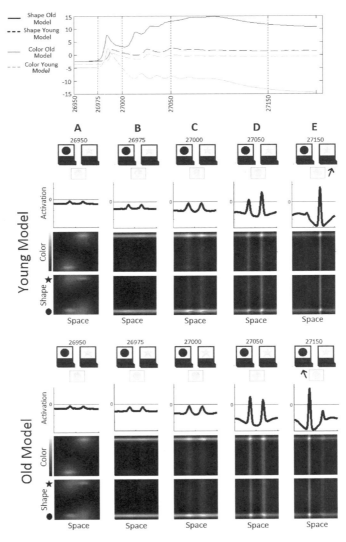

FIGURE 7.—A zoom-in on the critical dynamics of the attentional system on a rule-switch trial is plotted at top for the "young" (dashed lines) and "old" (solid lines) models. The middle panel shows the object working memory (WM) system for the "young" model while the bottom panel shows the object WM system for the "old" model. Panel A shows the object WM systems at the beginning of the post-switch phase. In Panel B the red circle test card is presented to the model. At the corresponding timestep in the top panel, the dimensional nodes for the old model have begun to separate, while the dimensional nodes for the "young" model both maintain activation near 0. In panel C, spatial activation begins to build at both spatial locations for the "young" and "old" models. In Panel D a decision is beginning to emerge as the rightward spatial location is more active for the "young" model but the leftward spatial location is more active for the "old" model. In Panel E both the "young" and "old" models have built a spatial response.

41

populations in the dorsal and ventral visual pathways. Through neural interactions within and between these populations, stable peaks of activation can emerge that capture decisions to sort objects (i.e., cards) to the left or right location in the DCCS task. Hebbian processes operating within these fields serve to accumulate memories over the course of the task, which can influence subsequent decisions.

To sort cards in a rule-like fashion, we introduced a frontal dimensional attention system that effectively boosts the baseline level of activity in the posterior neural fields (e.g., Egner & Hirsch, 2005; Lepsien & Nobre, 2007; Zanto et al., 2010, 2011). In addition, we implemented a specific type of developmental change in the dimensional attention system to capture the emergence of rule-use between 3 and 5 years: the older model had stronger excitatory and inhibitory neural interactions in the frontal system and a more precise pattern of connectivity with the posterior system. As a consequence, the 3-year-old model perseverated: this model was not able to achieve robust activation of the "shape" node; consequently, cooperation in the color field dominated the sorting decision. By contrast, the 5-year-old model switched rules: this model robustly activated the "shape" node, boosted the baseline activity in the shape field, and correctly sorted the red circle to the circle target card on the left. Interestingly, the different dynamics of the dimensional attention system for the young and old models in Figure 7 could explain the fNIRS data from Moriguchi and Hiraki (2009). Specifically, the older model that switches rules shows much stronger "frontal" activation compared to the young model. This parallels the pattern of data for switchers and perseverators in Moriguchi and Hiraki (2009). We discuss these ties in greater detail in the General Discussion (Chapter VII).

The DNF model is clearly a model of children's performance in the DCCS task. But is it more than that? At face value, the answer to this question is certainly "yes." Recall that the DNF model builds on an earlier model of how children and adults "bind" visual features together (see, Johnson et al., 2008; Spencer, Austin et al., 2012). Thus, the model speaks to issues that extend beyond the purview of the DCCS task (for a more detailed discussion, see Chapter VII). Moreover, the model implementation makes specific claims about the general nature of rule-use and executive control. For instance, there was no explicit representation of the rules in the model. Rather, rule-use emerged from specific associations of features with spatial locations in an object WM system and the associations of dimensional attention nodes with cortical populations in the object system. This means that the "rule" does not reside in the frontal system—that system knows nothing about the specific test card presented or where the target cards are in the task space. These details are "known" in the object system; however, the object system knows nothing about the meaning of the "color" or "shape" game. Thus, rule-use—and the ability to switch rules—emerges from interactions across multiple neural populations.

We can also ask how the different components of EF—inhibitory control, working memory, and task-switching—are captured by the model. For instance, how does the model inhibit irrelevant information? This is partly the job of the dimensional attention system, for instance, boosting the excitation of the "color" node on the first pre-switch trial in the color game. But inhibitory processes also play a role: when the "color" node was boosted, lateral inhibitory interactions suppressed the activity of the "shape" node. Inhibitory processes were also at work in the posterior neural fields. Here, the build-up of activation in the color field at the left location increased the activation of neurons on the left side of the shape field. As this activation increased in the shape field, laterally inhibitory interactions suppressed activation associated with the star feature at the rightward location, binding the test card features to the left location. Thus, inhibitory control—a key cognitive concept in early development—emerges from excitatory neural processes (e.g., boosting the "color" node) and associated laterally inhibitory consequences (e.g., suppressing the "shape" node; for related ideas, see Morton & Munakata, 2002; Roberts et al., 1994; Roberts & Pennington, 1996; Stedron et al., 2005).

Similar processes have been used to explain inhibitory control in the Simon task. In this task, the spatial location of the stimulus can either be congruent or incongruent with the spatial response required for the stimulus. To simulate this task, Erlhagen and Schöner (2002) gave a DNF model stimuli that either overlapped (as in a congruent trial) or conflicted with one another (as in an incongruent trial). When an incongruent stimulus was presented, it was inhibited through lateral inhibition generated by the build-up of excitation associated with the relevant response location. Thus, activation peaks and inhibitory processes go hand-in-hand.

What about a second component of EF—where does "switching" live in our DNF model? There were many components of the model's dynamics that produced rule-switching. This required a strong representation of the relevant dimension brought about through robust activation of the relevant dimensional neuron. This, in turn, produced a strong boost to a specific feature-space field, helping this field resolve the conflict between the task input at one location and the Hebbian trace at another location. But the full resolution of this conflict required building excitation at the "correct" feature value in the feature-space field and suppressing the incorrect feature via lateral inhibition. Switching, then, requires a confluence of robust neural activation peaks and lateral inhibitory processes.

These examples are informative in that they highlight the challenge of relating cognitive concepts such as "inhibitory control" and "task-switching" to mechanisms in a neural model, and the utility of having a neural model to bridge between these two levels of description. Our simulations show that the DNF model can produce functional behavioral outcomes central to cognitive control in early development such as changes in the ability to switch tasks and inhibit a prepotent response. But these outcomes do not map one-to-one onto specific neural mechanisms. That is, there is not an inhibitory module or a task-switching module in the model; rather, the model helps explain how functional behaviors labeled as, for instance, "inhibitory control" can arise from neural mechanisms in a complex neural system.

For this link between cognitive concepts and neural mechanisms to have meaning, however, we must first demonstrate the utility of the theory. We do this in the following sections by quantitatively simulating a host of behavioral effects in the literature. Next, we generate a set of novel behavioral predictions and test these predictions with 3-year-old children. Critically, these predictions are not consistent with any other theory of children's performance in the DCCS task. We then demonstrate that the DNF model can capture several additional findings from a study that present a challenge to other theories, thereby showing how the DNF model speaks to a wide range of issues central to the early development of executive function. We conclude in Chapter VII by returning to the early development of EF and asking what the model contributes to our understanding of this critically important topic.

NOTES

1. Note that neural population dynamics within two-dimensional neural fields have the same properties discussed above, except now lateral neural interactions occur along both dimensions. This creates a "Mexican-hat" profile with a peak of excitation surrounded by a circular trough of inhibition. Note also that each WM field in Figure 4 consists of an excitatory layer that forms Hebbian memories and a layer of inhibitory interneurons. For simplicity, we only show activation in the excitatory layer in all figures.

2. Note that the fronto-parietal connections did not play a role in the simulations reported here. Consequently, we do not discuss them further, although studies show developmental changes in fronto-parietal connectivity during childhood (Crone, Donohue, et al., 2006).

3. It is important to note that the strength of the Hebbian memories do not grow stronger than the influence of the target inputs. That is, the model always has access to the "correct" information within each individual field. For example, if the model were given a unidimensional post-switch feature, activation would be stronger at the location of the target input compared to the location of the Hebbian memory, and the model would build a peak of activation at the location of the target input.

IV. QUANTITATIVE FITS OF CORE FINDINGS IN THE DCCS LITERATURE

In this section, we present—for the first time—quantitative simulations of a diverse array of findings from the literature on children's performance in the DCCS task. Specifically, we show that the DNF model reproduces the pattern of data across versions of the task that manipulate the features between the pre-switch and post-switch phases, as well as versions that manipulate the degree of conflict during the pre-switch phase. These variants of the task have played a central role in evaluating existing theories of children's performance. Thus, the simulation results in this section establish that the DFT achieves extensive coverage of the extant literature at a level of quantitative detail that has not yet been achieved by any other theory.

In the previous section, we described how the model can autonomously sort cards by modulating the resting level of populations of neurons tuned to specific features. This was accomplished through the neural dynamics in an autonomous dimensional attention system that was coupled to the feature fields. Figure 8A shows these neural dynamics in action in a simple variant of the DCCS task with only two pre-switch trials and two post-switch trials (to enable a close-up view of the activation profiles). As noted previously, there are critical differences between the activation of the nodes during the pre- and post-switch phases. Recall that during the pre-switch phase, the "color" node is boosted by a fixed amount, reflecting the task instructions "let's play the color game." During the post-switch phase, the boost is applied in reverse, that is, the "shape" node is now boosted by the same fixed amount (i.e., "let's play the shape game"). Notice in Figure 8A, however, that even though the boost amount is the same strength in the post-switch phase, the shape node activation is lower than the color node activation from the pre-switch phase. Reversely, the color node activation in the post-switch phase is greater than the shape node activation from the pre-switch phase. These two effects are the result of Hebbian memories accumulated for the "color" node during the pre-switch phase. The Hebbian traces boost the color node in the post-switch phase and slightly suppress the shape node activation due to lateral inhibition.

In the simulations described below, we simplified the neural dynamics within the dimensional attention system to make the task of quantitatively

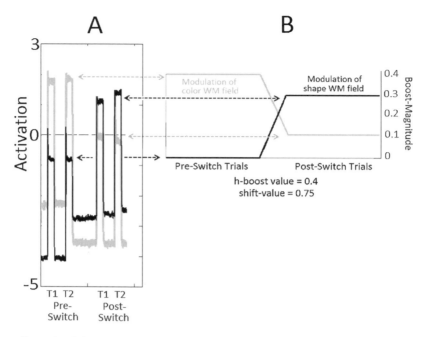

FIGURE 8.—Schematic diagram depicting the simplified processes of boosting and shifting. The boost value applied to the shape (black line) or color (gray line) working memory (WM) fields is plotted to the right. For trials 1–6, the boost (0.4) is applied to the pre-switch field (the color WM field) is the full boost value. At trial 7 a portion of the boost is shifted to post-switch field (the shape WM field) determined by the shift value (0.75). The grounding of this schematic is shown in the alignment to the activation of the dimensional neurons for the young model. This represents normalizing the boost value to the activation of the shape neuron during the pre-switch phase.

simulating results from many studies in the literature tractable. In particular, we replaced the autonomous dimensional attention system with two nodes that passed static activation values to the posterior neural system during the pre- and post-switch phases. This eliminated the rise and fall dynamics of the dimensional attention system evident in Figure 8A, but retained the key consequence of these neural dynamics—a boost in the baseline level of activation in a particular feature field, and a reduction in the fidelity of this boost during the post-switch phase.

We used two parameters to specify the activation passed from the dimensional nodes to the feature fields. First, we used a *boost* parameter that specified the strength of the global boost, effectively the global difference in activation of the cued versus non-cued dimensions in each phase of the task. The 3-year-old model used small boost values to reflect the weak neural interactions within the dimensional attention system and the imprecise connectivity between the dimensional nodes and the feature fields, while the 5-year-old model used larger boost values. Second, we used a *shift* parameter that specified the fidelity or proportion of the boost applied during the post-switch phase (with 1.0 reflecting a perfect shift in attention and 0.0 reflecting no shift in attention). The 3-year-old model used smaller shift values, reflecting the difficulty this model had overcoming the Hebbian traces from the pre-switch phase to selectively activate a single dimensional node during the post-switch phase. The 5-year-old model used larger shift values, reflecting a more complete shift in dimensional attention (see, e.g., the bottom panel of Figure 6).

Figure 8B shows an example of the simplified dimensional attention system. In this example, the boost value is 0.4 and the shift value is 0.75. Thus, on the pre-switch trials (Pre-Switch T1 and T2 along the *x*-axis), the resting level of the color field was boosted by 0.4 units, while the shape field remained at baseline. This captures the quantitative difference in activation between the color and shape nodes during the pre-switch trials shown in Figure 8A. On the post-switch trials (Post-Switch T1 and T2 along the *x*-axis), we applied the shift value. Thus, on trial 7, 75% of the boost value ($0.4 \times 0.75 = 0.3$) was applied to the post-switch field—the shape field—while the remaining 25% remained with the color field. Again, this reflects the quantitative difference in activation between the color and shape nodes during the post-switch trials shown in Figure 8A.

The final assumption we made when selecting the parameters of the dimensional attention system for the 3- and 5-year-old models was that individual children differ in their ability to attend to particular dimensions. This creates a continuum of individual abilities across the two age groups. Conceptually, then, there is not one optimal boost and shift parameter to describe all 3-year-olds and a different optimal boost and shift parameter to describe all 5-year-olds. Rather, some 3-year-olds, for example, might show an enhanced ability to boost attention to one feature dimension relative to their peers. Thus, to capture developmental differences between 3 and 5 years, we used the two *boost distributions* shown in Figure 9. As this figure shows, the 3-year-old model had a mean boost value of 0.35 and the 5-year-old model had a mean boost of 0.5. This reflects the increase in the strength of neural interactions in the dimensional attention system, as well as an increase in the precision of the connectivity between the frontal and posterior systems. We also used two *shift distributions* (see Figure 10). The 3-year-old distribution encompassed a broad range of values centered on 0.5 while the 5-year-old distribution was skewed more toward values between 0.6 and 1. This reflects an increase in the efficiency with which children are able to switch attention and overcome Hebbian traces accumulated during the pre-switch phase. Note that the boost and shift values were selected independently for each simulation based on the age-specific probability distributions shown in

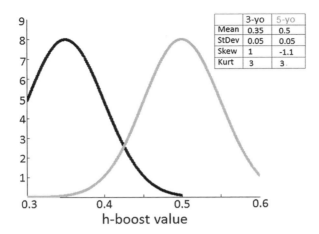

	3-yo	5-yo
Mean	0.35	0.5
StDev	0.05	0.05
Skew	1	-1.1
Kurt	3	3.

h-boost value

FIGURE 9.—H-boost distributions for 3- and 5-year-old models. The distribution for 3-year-olds is dominated by lower h-boost values, while the distribution for 5-year-olds is dominated by higher h-boost values reflecting the stronger mapping of the dimensional nodes to their relevant feature fields.

Figures 9 and 10. This provides a conservative starting point for probing the development of flexible rule-use in our model in that we made no assumptions about how the ability to boost attention to one dimension was related to the ability to switch the attentional focus with high fidelity.

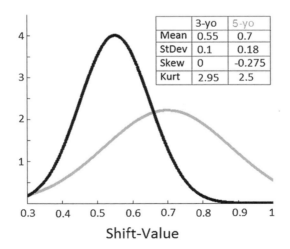

	3-yo	5-yo
Mean	0.55	0.7
StDev	0.1	0.18
Skew	0	-0.275
Kurt	2.95	2.5

Shift-Value

FIGURE 10.—Shift-value distributions for 3- and 5-year-old models. The 3-year-old distribution covers a wide range of intermediary value while the 5-year-old distribution is skewed to values closer to 1 capturing the increasing fidelity with which the dimensional nodes are able to achieve robust selective activation.

In the sections that follow, we describe our simulation method in detail, including how we identified the set of final parameters used and constraints on model parameters. We then turn to quantitative simulations of results from the DCCS literature.

Method

Simulations were conducted in Matlab 7.5.0 (The Mathworks, Inc., Natick, Massachusettes, United States) on a PC with an Intel® i7™ 3.33 GHz quad-core processor (the Matlab code is available from the authors on request). *The same model parameters were used for all conditions*; the only differences across simulations were the inputs presented to the model to reflect differences in the DCCS tasks that were simulated.

For all simulations, the model was given six test cards (three of each possible combination of features) for both the pre- and post-switch phases. Throughout each simulation, target inputs were presented at specific feature and spatial values to capture the relevant details of the target cards for the pre- and post-switch phases. At the start of each trial, the model was presented with ridges of input for the features present on the test card. The model's response on each trial was determined based on the location (left or right tray) of the peak in the spatial field. For example, if the model made a decision to sort a card to the left tray, then it would bind the features on the test card to the left location in the feature fields and build a corresponding peak of activation at the left location in the spatial field. Thus, the model generates a "left" or "right" decision on every trial. The model is scored as correct based on the spatial location of the target inputs to the shape and color feature fields and the "game" being played (color game or shape game).

Each trial was simulated for 1,500 timesteps, with the test card stimulus presented for 1,000 timesteps. The model always generated a response by the end of the 1,500 timestep interval. Next, we decreased the resting-level of the WM fields to destabilize any peaks and prepare the field for the subsequent presentation of a test card. For all of the figures and simulation examples in the Results Section, color is the pre-switch dimension and shape is the post-switch dimension.

Three batches of 100 simulations (i.e., 100 children) were conducted for each condition for each age group to get rates of perseveration and switching for quantitative fits. As in the literature, the model was required to sort at least five out of six pre-switch test cards correctly. Further, a model was characterized as passing if five or more post-switch test cards were correctly sorted and as failing if 1 or fewer post-switch cards were sorted correctly. The model parameters can be found in the Appendix. As noted previously, these parameters were held constant for all simulations in both age groups.

The best fitting parameters were assessed en masse across all conditions. An initial set of parameters was generated to fit the Standard condition, which was then tested across all conditions. Parameters were modified in an iterative fashion in order to maximize the fit across all conditions. There were various constraints imposed on the parameters of the model. For example, the dynamics of the object WM were tuned to reliably form peaks of activation across all WM fields. Further, the parameters of the Hebbian learning process were constrained to not grow larger than the target inputs and to still allow for correct switching with strong dimensional attention.

Results

Grounding rule-use in a process-based model that generates active responses on every trial imposes robust constraints when trying to capture the details of 3- and 5-year-olds' performance. First, because we simulated both the pre- and post-switch phases, the model must show high levels of correct sorting during the initial sorting phase. More importantly, the model must also capture the all-or-none aspect of children's performance during the post-switch phase. That is, the model must either completely perseverate and sort all of the cards incorrectly, or completely switch and successfully sort all of the cards correctly. The literature reveals a very specific pattern of results depending on the presence or absence of conflict and different changes to the features on the cards. In the following section, we show that the model is able to quantitatively capture these details.

Standard Version

The first issue we probed was whether the model quantitatively captures children's performance in the Standard DCCS task. Figure 11A shows the rates of perseveration and switching for the model and literature sampled for 3- and 5-year-olds (Halford et al., 2007; Müller et al., 2006; Zelazo, Frye, & Rapus, 1996; Zelazo et al., 2003). As can be seen, the model exhibits a high rate of perseveration similar to 3-year-olds and also closely matches the level of correct switching for 5-year-olds. As discussed above, the only difference between these simulations across age is the strength of the *boost* for each age group and the *shift* of the resting-level modulation between the pre- and post-switch phases.

The top panel in Figure 11A explains why the 3-year-old model perseverates. Going into the post-switch phase, there is cooperation of Hebbian memories and target inputs in the color field (the pre-switch field). That is, the model has always sorted red test cards to the right and blue test cards to the left. By contrast, there are competing Hebbian memories and target inputs in the shape field (the post-switch field): the model is "seeing" a star on the right and a circle on the left, but has Hebbian memories at the opposite locations. In this circumstance, the model requires a strong boost to

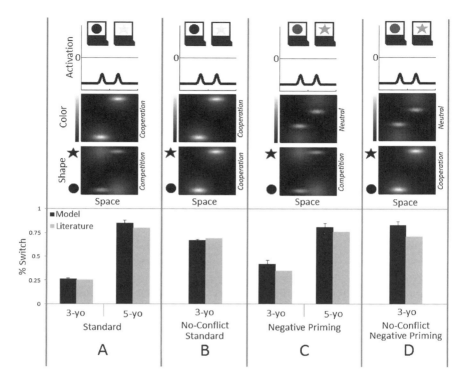

FIGURE 11.—Working memory (WM) fields of the model at the beginning of the post-switch phase and simulation results for the Standard version (Panel A), No-Conflict Standard version (Panel B), Negative Priming version (Panel C), and the No-Conflict Negative Priming version (Panel D).

the shape field to overcome the competition and sort by the post-switch dimension. The weak boost of the shape field for the 3-year-old model is not up to the task—this boost is not sufficient to inhibit the cooperative bias in the color field. The 5-year-old model, on the other hand, has a stronger boost and higher fidelity switch. This activates the shape field more robustly and the color field more weakly, allowing the model to correctly sort by the post-switch rules.

No-Conflict Standard Version

Can the pattern of cooperation and competition within the feature-space fields generalize beyond the Standard version? One version reviewed above examined the role of conflict during the pre-switch phase. This study showed that the post-switch performance of 3-year-olds significantly improved if the test cards match the target cards along both dimensions during the pre-switch phase (Zelazo et al., 2003). Eliminating this conflict should have a similar impact on the model's performance. Figure 11B shows simulation results of

51

the young model and data with 3-year-olds (Zelazo et al., 2003). The model quantitatively reproduces the relatively high switching rate displayed by 3-year-olds—both models and children sort correctly over 60% of the time.

As can be seen in the top panel, no-conflict cards during the pre-switch phase establish cooperation in both the color and shape fields. That is, going into the post-switch phase, the inputs for the target cards overlap with Hebbian memories established during the pre-switch phase. Although there is still overlap of Hebbian memories and target inputs in the color field, there is no longer competition in the shape field. Thus, the 3-year-old model with only a weak boost is able to correctly bind the test cards to locations based on shape. This shows how memories for the spatial layout of features can eliminate the need for inhibition, influencing the amount of boost required to successfully sort during the post-switch phase.

Negative Priming Version

Our simulations of the standard condition indicate that there are two key factors that play a role in 3-year-olds' perseverative behavior—(1) overlap between Hebbian memories and target inputs in the pre-switch field and (2) conflict between Hebbian memories and target inputs in the post-switch field. That is, the model is affected by conflict between what it remembers, and what it "sees." One question is whether each source plays a central role. This is addressed in the Negative Priming version where the features that were relevant during the pre-switch phase are changed in the post-switch phase.

Figure 11C shows quantitative fits of the model with this version of the task where the colors were changed in the post-switch phase. Like the empirical data (Müller et al., 2006; Zelazo et al., 2003), the 3-year-old model shows a high rate of perseveration and the 5-year-old model shows a high rate of switching. The top panel in Figure 11C shows the model just before the start of the post-switch phase. Now, new target inputs are present in the color field at the values for yellow and green (see the shift in the positions of the light gray ovals between, for instance, Figure 11B, C). These new color values do not overlap with the Hebbian traces for red and blue; thus, the color field has a neutral degree of cooperation/competition. There is, however, still competition in the shape field. As before, this competition slows peak building in the shape field during the post-switch trials. Consequently, peaks first emerge in the color field and the 3-year-old model perseveratively sorts by this dimension. Thus, perseveration at 3 years can emerge solely due to competition in the post-switch field. The 5-year-old model overcomes this competition with a stronger resting-level boost to the shape field.

No-Conflict Negative Priming Version

The No-Conflict Negative Priming version verifies that conflict along the post-switch dimension is the critical source of error in the Negative Priming version. This version eliminates the post-switch conflict by asking children to sort test cards that match the target cards along both color and shape dimensions during the pre-switch phase. Results from this version are shown in Figure 11D. As in the Negative Priming version, there are new target inputs (green, yellow) for the color dimension at the start of the post-switch trial, creating a neutral state in the color field. Now, however, there are overlapping Hebbian memories and target inputs in the shape field because the model sorted no-conflict cards during the pre-switch phase. This creates cooperation in the shape field, eliminating the need for inhibition of the Hebbian memories. Thus, the 3-year-old model, like children, is able to switch rules (Müller et al., 2006; Zelazo et al., 2003).

Partial-Change Version

The Partial-Change version is the opposite of the Negative Priming version in that it probes whether cooperation in the pre-switch field is sufficient to drive children's errors. In this version, the features for the post-switch dimension are changed while the features for the pre-switch dimension remain constant throughout the procedure. As can be seen in the top panel of Figure 12A, changing the shape features going into the first post-switch trial eliminates conflict in the shape field, creating a neutral degree of cooperation/competition. There is, however, still overlap between Hebbian memories and target inputs in the color field. As the simulation results show, this cooperation is sufficient to drive perseveration with only a weak boost provided to the color field. In particular, activation builds more quickly in the color field and the model, like children, tends to perseverate (Zelazo et al., 2003).

Total-Change Version

In the Total-Change version, all of the features that were present during the pre-switch phase are changed for the post-switch phase. Thus, as can be seen in the top panel of Figure 12B, this version eliminates both the cooperation in the color field and the competition in the shape field, creating a neutral state in both. Simulation results show that the model, like 3-year-olds, does not perseverate in the Total-Change version (Zelazo et al., 2003). Thus, even though the 3-year-old model has just a small boost in the resting level of the shape field on the post-switch trials, this is sufficient—in this condition—to correctly switch rules.

Relational Complexity Version

The relational complexity version examines the role of the relational propositions that must be represented in a hierarchical rule-structure in, for instance, CCC/CCC-r theory. This was accomplished by reducing the number of irrelevant features during the pre- and post-switch phases (see Figure 1G). Here, children received two conflict and two no-conflict test cards and were scored as passing if they sorted all four post-switch cards correctly. Figure 12C

53

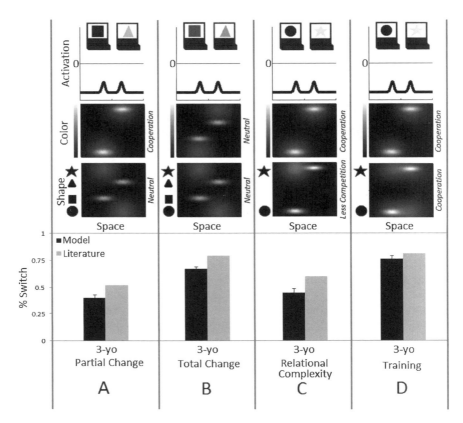

FIGURE 12.—Working memory (WM) fields for the model at the beginning of the post-switch phase and simulation results for the Partial-Change version (Panel A), Total-Change version (Panel B), Relational Complexity version (Panel C), and the training study by Brace et al. (2006; Panel D).

shows that 3-year-olds—and the model—show better switching performance in this version relative to the standard task (Halford et al., 2007). As can be seen in the top panel of Figure 12C, the relational complexity version reduces competition in the shape field at the beginning of the post-switch phase because there is only conflict for one of the post-switch features. This reduced competition allows a weak representation of the rules to guide more accurate rule-use.

Training Version

Brace et al. (2006) showed that 3-year-olds' post-switch performance was improved when they were given a training phase between the pre- and post-switch phases. Specifically, they gave children a series of cards that started with images that contained only the post-switch features. Over a series of 6 training trials, the pre-switch features were gradually "morphed" from a neutral image into the fully bivalent stimuli at which point the post-switch phase began.

We administered this training task to the model in the same fashion. The model was given six pre-switch trials. At the start of the training phase, the model was given only a post-switch feature. Over the six training cards, the strength of the pre-switch inputs were increased to reflect the increasing salience and specificity of the pre-switch features as they were "morphed" into the bivalent stimuli. As can be seen in Figure 12D, the model benefited from this training phase in a manner similar to 3-year-olds. Specifically, 83% of the models were able to correctly switch rules compared to 88% of 3-year-olds averaged across the Training and Training-Plus-Instructions conditions reported by Brace et al. (2006). In the DNF model, similar to the PDP model of Morton and Munakata (2002), this benefit resulted from the formation of Hebbian memories in the shape field during the training phase that overlapped with the post-switch target features. This reduced the competition in the shape field, allowing the young model to switch rules.

Summary of Quantitative Fits

A central innovation of the DNF model is that it integrates the dynamics of object representation with a simple form of dimensional attention—boosting the resting level of different neural populations when cued by the label "shape" or "color." The strength of the model in generalizing across conditions stemmed from the ability of the model to bind features and form Hebbian memories associating features with spatial locations. As the pattern of competition and cooperation in the color and shape fields changed across conditions, this tipped the balance toward perseveration or correct performance in the context of activation provided by the dimensional attention system. Thus, critical aspects of children's performance across conditions came "for free" from these details.

Although the model captured the quantitative details of children's performance across conditions, this was not guaranteed a priori. Indeed, the effort to "tune" the model's parameters revealed multiple constraints posed by the pattern of behavioral data. For instance, the initial "boost" value provided to the model had to be strong enough to drive correct rule-use during pre-switch phase, but not so strong that the model would always show correct performance in the post-switch phase. Similarly, the combination of the boost and shift parameters had to be weak enough (i.e., a "shift" value < 0.5) to produce some perseveration in situations where cooperation in the post-switch field biased the model to respond correctly. For example, it proved challenging to move the model off ceiling performance (100% correct) in the No-Conflict Negative Priming version.

In total, the simulations reported here quantitatively simulated children's performance from eight different variants of the DCCS task all with the same parameters, including two variants reporting data from both 3- and 5-year-olds. Note that our ability to simulate 5-year-olds' performance was limited by the fact that the majority of studies in the literature do not report data for this age group. We note, however, that the 5-year-old model does, in fact, switch correctly in all variants of the task reported here. Note also that the four developmental parameters we changed to create the 5-year-old model were all necessary to achieve accurate switching performance. Changing only the mean of the boost or shift distributions, for instance, produced high levels of intermediate switching (i.e., sorting between two or four out of six cards correctly during the post-switch phase). Thus, the number of parameters changed over development was necessary to capture the specific pattern of rule-switching present in the literature.

The simulations presented here demonstrate that the DNF model provides an integrative account of young children's performance in the DCCS task that can capture a broad array of findings in the literature. This is one key role of formal theories—to bring together a diverse set of empirical results in a single, unified framework. But this is only one function of formal theories. A second function is to use theories to generate novel, sometimes counterintuitive predictions that are not consistent with other theories in the literature. Chapter V pursues this second goal.

V. EMPIRICAL TEST OF THE DNF MODEL: THE ROLE OF SPACE

The model we have presented is able to achieve extensive coverage of the existing literature through the interaction of spatially specific memories for features and a simple form of dimensional attention. Critically, all of the effects simulated above emerged from spatially specific competition or cooperation between target inputs and Hebbian memories in different feature fields. This leads to the prediction that the DCCS task is not just about "rules"—*space should also matter*. Spatial information is not an aspect of any theory of EF, rule-use, or the DCCS task. And, as we highlight next, the spatial properties of the DNF model predict that we can reverse two known effects in the literature *simply by moving where the target cards are located in the task space.* Note that we are not claiming the DCCS task is *only* about space, an issue we will return to later. Rather, in the present section, we highlight a key way in which our theory diverges from all others and generates a set of counterintuitive predictions.

To test whether space plays a role in children's rule-use in the DCCS task, we constructed two new experimental conditions based on the No-Conflict Negative Priming and the Negative Priming versions simulated above. In the No-Conflict Negative Priming version, there is cooperation within the post-switch feature field and 3-year-olds are able to switch rules, while in the Negative Priming version there is competition in the post-switch feature field and 3-year-olds perseverate. Critically, if the layout of Hebbian memories and target inputs in these two versions is indeed the source of 3-year-olds' success and failure, *then swapping the spatial locations of the target cards before the post-switch trials should reverse this pattern of results.*

Recall that in the No-Conflict Negative Priming version (Müller et al., 2006; Zelazo et al., 2003) the test cards match the target cards along both dimensions during the pre-switch phase and the features that are relevant for the pre-switch phase are changed before the start of the post-switch phase. Figure 13A shows the model of the No-Conflict Negative Priming version reproduced here for ease of comparison. The 3-year-old model is able to switch in this version because there is cooperation in the shape field and a neutral state in the color field. What happens in our "Space Swap" version of this task shown in Figure 13B? This version swaps the locations of the target

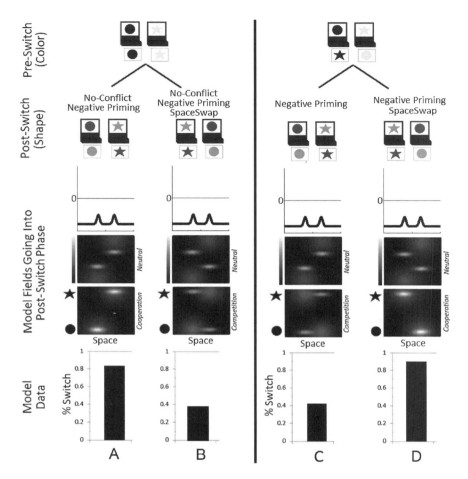

FIGURE 13.—Model at the start of the pre-switch phase for the No-Conflict Negative Priming (Panel A) and No-Conflict Negative Priming-SpaceSwap versions (Panel B). In this example, color is the pre-switch dimension and shape is the post-switch dimension. In panel B, conflict is introduced in the post-switch (shape) working memory (WM) field by swapping the locations of the target cards. The bottom panel shows the data from the 3-year-old DNF model. Also shown is the model at the start of the pre-switch phase for the Negative Priming (Panel C) and Negative Priming SpaceSwap versions (Panel D). In this example, color is the pre-switch dimension and shape is the post-switch dimension. In Panel D conflict is eliminated in the post-switch (shape) WM field by swapping the locations of the target cards. The bottom panel shows the simulated data from the 3-year-old dynamic neural field (DNF) model.

cards (see post-switch display). Consequently, there is now competition between Hebbian memories and target inputs in the shape field, and 3-year-olds should have more difficulty switching rules. Simulation results in the bottom panel confirm this prediction. Thus, 3-year-olds in the No-Conflict

Negative Priming-SpaceSwap version should perseverate, while 3-year-olds in the No-Conflict Negative Priming version should switch correctly. This is striking because everything is identical in these versions—the rule structure, the target cards, the test cards—*except the location of the target cards during the post-switch phase.*

In the Negative Priming version (Müller et al., 2006; Zelazo et al., 2003), on the other hand, there is conflict between the test cards and target cards during the pre-switch phase (see pre-switch display in Figure 13C) and the features that were relevant for the pre-switch game are changed for the post-switch game (see post-switch display in Figure 13D). Recall that in this version, 3-year-olds perseverate. The model also perseverated in the Negative Priming version because of the competition in the shape field (see middle panel of Figure 13C). Figure 13D illustrates the effect of swapping the spatial locations of the target cards in the Negative Priming version. As before, the locations of the target cards have been swapped at the start of the post-switch phase (see post-switch display). Consequently, in Figure 13D the locations of the target inputs now overlap with the Hebbian memories in the shape field, which should facilitate rule-switching in 3-year-olds. Simulation results in the bottom panel confirm this prediction. Thus, the model predicts that 3-year-olds in the Negative Priming-SpaceSwap version should switch rules, even though everything—the rule structure, the target cards, the test cards—is identical relative to the Negative Priming version *except the location of the target cards during the post-switch phase.*

Simulation results in the bottom panel of Figure 13 summarize the key predictions across conditions. The No-Conflict Negative Priming version shows high rates of switching, but the model predicts that children will perseverate in this condition when we swap the spatial location of the target cards in the post-switch phase. By contrast, the Negative Priming version shows high rates of perseveration. Here, the model predicts that children will switch correctly in this condition when we swap the spatial location of the test cards in the post-switch phase. Thus, the model predicts that simply swapping the locations of the target cards will push performance in opposite directions for these two conditions. Importantly, the features and rules remain the same in all versions of the task; therefore *all other existing theories predict that the space-swap manipulation should have no impact on children's performance.* We tested the DNF predictions in the following experiment.

Method

Participants

Seventy-six 3-year-olds between 38 and 46 months of age ($M = 41.67$ months, $SD = 2.68$ months) were included in the final analysis ($N = 19$ for all four groups). An additional nine children were dropped due to experimenter error ($N=4$), failing to pass the pre-switch phase (i.e., sort at least four cards correctly, see Zelazo et al., 2003; $N=3$), or parental interference ($N=2$).

Materials

The pre-switch target cards for all versions were a red star at the right location and a blue circle at the left location. The pre-switch test cards for the No-Conflict Negative Priming versions were red stars and blue circles. The pre-switch test cards for the Negative Priming versions were red circles and blue stars. Depending on the task-order, the post-switch cards were either red and blue triangles and squares (for the shape-color task order), or green and yellow stars and circles (for the color-shape task order). In the Space-Swap versions, the locations of the target cards were swapped for the post-switch phase (see Figure 13). For all versions, five pre-switch and five post-switch test cards were used with no more than three of any particular card appearing in any sorting phase.

Procedure

Sessions were run individually with the child and experimenter in a quiet room. The experimenter began by showing the cards to the child and saying that they were going to play a couple of games. The experimenter stated the name of the first game, how the cards were to be sorted, and the specific rules for that game. For example, the experimenter said, "First, we are going to play the color game. In the color game, we sort the cards by color. So, all of the red ones go here and all of the blue ones go there." The experimenter then demonstrated a card for each rule saying, for example, "See, this one is red so it goes here." The experimenter presented the test cards one at a time to the child. When presenting a card, the experimenter did not provide a label but asked, "Where does this one go in the color game?"

After the pre-switch cards had been sorted, the experimenter stated that they were all done with that game and were going to play a new game. In all conditions, the experimenter then removed the target cards and replaced them with the post-switch target cards, stated the name of the new game, how the cards were now to be sorted, and the specific rules for the new game just as in the pre-switch. No demonstration of the post-switch rules was supplied. The post-switch test cards were presented just as in the pre-switch. Throughout both phases, no direct feedback was provided. If the child incorrectly sorted a card, the experimenter simply reminded the child of the rules by saying, for example, "Remember, we are playing the color game, so we are sorting the cards by color. All of the red ones go here and all of the blue ones go there." Note that *the space swap conditions were identical to the standard conditions except for a single change*—after the target cards were removed at the end of the pre-switch phase, they were repositioned at the opposite spatial locations.

Results

Children were categorized as passing the post-switch phase if they sorted at least four out of five cards correctly and as failing if they sorted one or fewer cards correctly (Zelazo et al., 2003). We removed data from the following children from further analysis for intermediate responding: two children in the No-Conflict Negative Priming version, zero children in the No-Conflict Negative Priming-SpaceSwap, three children in the Negative Priming condition, and one child in the Negative Priming-SpaceSwap condition. The percent of children who correctly switched rules in each condition is shown in Figure 14, along with the predictions from model simulations.

The first question we examined was whether data from the No Swap conditions replicated previous findings. This was indeed the case: Significantly more children in the Negative Priming group failed to switch rules than in the No-Conflict Negative Priming group ($\chi^2(1) = 10.186$, $p = 0.001$). Next, we tested the predictions of the DNF model by comparing the No-Conflict Negative Priming and No-Conflict Negative Priming-SpaceSwap conditions (see Figure 14A). As predicted, significantly more children failed to switch rules in the No-Conflict Negative Priming-SpaceSwap condition than in the No-Conflict Negative Priming condition ($\chi^2(1) = 3.995$, $p = 0.04$). We then tested the other prediction of the DNF model by comparing the Negative Priming and the Negative Priming-SpaceSwap conditions (see Figure 14B). Again as predicted, significantly more children failed to switch rules in the Negative Priming version than in the Negative Priming-SpaceSwap version ($\chi^2(1) = 4.48$, $p = 0.03$).

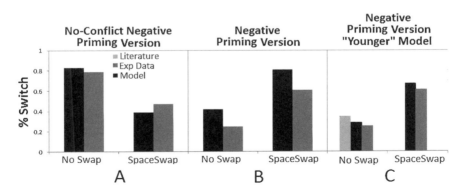

FIGURE 14.—Children's performance and dynamic neural field (DNF) model data. Panel A shows the No-Conflict Negative Priming and No-Conflict Negative Priming-SpaceSwap conditions. Panel B shows the Negative Priming and Negative Priming SpaceSwap conditions. Panel C shown data from less developmentally advanced 3-year-old model (only the bottom 87% of the *shift* and *boost* distributions were analyzed).

Results from the present study showed that a simple manipulation of the spatial structure of the DCCS task can have surprising effects on the behavior of 3-year-olds. Specifically, by swapping the location of the target cards between the pre- and post-switch phases, we reversed the pattern of results from the No-Conflict Negative Priming and Negative Priming versions. Three-year-olds typically switch rules in the No-Conflict Negative Priming version; however, swapping the locations of the target cards significantly impaired their performance. Three-year-olds typically perseverate in the Negative Priming version; however, swapping the locations of the target cards significantly improved their performance. The DNF model predicted this reversal of the behavioral effects from each condition a priori; no other theory provides an account of such effects because the features and rules are identical in the standard and space-swap variants of the task.

For example, according to CCC/CCC-r theory, children perseverate in the Negative Priming version due to the suppression of the post-switch rules, not due to any learning about where the post-switch features are sorted. Thus, it should not matter where the post-switch features are positioned in the task space. By contrast, the PDP model proposed by Morton and Munakata (2002) only learns about the relevant dimension on the pre-switch trials, that is, the feature dimension that is most strongly activated. Consequently, there are no weight changes associated with the post-switch features that could guide differential performance across the standard and space-swap conditions. Moreover, the spatial positions of the cards are not captured in the PDP model in any grounded way; rather, the mapping between the output units and space is built-in a priori. As such, there is no clear way to implement our manipulation in this model.

One potential concern with our findings, however, is the quantitative difference between the model predictions and the behavioral data from the Negative Priming and Negative Priming-SpaceSwap conditions: children in these conditions underperformed (i.e., lower percent switching) relative to the model predictions (see Figure 14B). One key observation regarding this discrepancy is shown in Figure 14C: children in our sample also underperformed relative to the data from the literature (Müller et al., 2006; Zelazo et al., 2003) that were used as an anchor point for our simulations (see light gray bar in Figure 14C).

Why did children in both the Negative Priming and Negative Priming-SpaceSwap conditions have such a hard time with these tasks? The age ranges in our conditions were comparable to previous studies, and we replicated the Negative Priming procedure exactly. A possible explanation for the quantitative difference across empirical samples is that we happened to sample from a group of less developmentally advanced 3-year-olds. To explore whether this could possibly yield the decrease in percent switching in *both* conditions, we reassessed the performance of the model, focusing only on the bottom 87% of the distributions of the boost and shift parameters, that is, focusing on parameters for the less developmentally advanced models. Simulation results from this analysis are plotted in Figure 14C (black bars). Data from the less developmentally advanced simulations more accurately fit the observed pattern of switching. Critically, this sampling bias in the model produced an equivalent decrement in *both Negative Priming and Negative Priming-SpaceSwap conditions*, effectively capturing the empirical pattern.

In summary, the data presented here demonstrate a critical role for spatial information in the DCCS task. What does this mean for EF in general? These data support the idea that EF emerges from the coupling between more abstract cognitive abilities like dimensional attention and basic processes such as working memory and response inhibition. In the latter case, our theory suggests that spatial information is critical to binding features together to make integrated object representations. The data reported here show that signatures of this spatial binding process show up in young children's ability— or inability—to flexibly shift tasks as the rules of the game change. Thus, spatial memories of where features should be placed in the task are not merely details that influence EF, but part of the processes that construct EF in the moment.

VI. BEYOND SPACE: THE ROLE OF FEATURE-SALIENCY AND ATTENTIONAL-WEIGHTS

The work we have presented thus far has highlighted the interaction of spatially specific featural information from the target cards and spatially specific Hebbian memories for features that accumulate as decisions are made. We turn now to new versions of the DCCS reported by Fisher (2011). These versions attempted to isolate the processes of voluntary and automatic shifts of attention by manipulating the saliency of dimensional features or the number of features per dimension. These versions provide a particularly useful probe of the DNF model because in this design the spatial locations of the target cards were randomized from trial to trial. Thus, these versions allow us to examine whether the DNF model can capture children's performance in tasks that are explicitly removed from spatial influences.

Feature-Saliency

In one set of conditions, Fisher (2011) manipulated the saliency of the features for each dimension. In this case, saliency was defined by similarity—that is, distinct or very different features were characterized as being more salient than similar features. This manipulation was motivated by two factors. First, previous research has shown that salient features automatically capture attention (Smith, Jones, & Landau, 1996; Treisman & Gelade, 1980). Thus, salient features facilitate an automatic shift of attention, while less salient features require a voluntary shift of attention. Second, data suggest that automatic attention is robust by 3 years of age, but voluntary attention is still developing (Fisher & Sloutsky, 2005; Smith et al., 1996). Based on these observations, Fisher (2011) proposed that changes in voluntary attention might play a critical role in the emergence of rule-use in the DCCS task. If this is the case, then post-switch trials that require a shift to a more salient dimension should be easier because such trials engage automatic attention. By contrast, a switch to a less salient dimension should be harder because this requires voluntary attention, which requires more effort.

To test this, Fisher (2011) used a version of the DCCS task with similar colors (red and pink) but distinct shapes. If voluntary attention is particularly hard for 3-year olds to recruit, they should have particular difficulty switching to color. Switching to shape, by contrast, should be automatic. Figure 15 shows the stimuli Fisher (2011) used. In addition to varying the salience of the stimuli, Fisher (2011) eliminated potential spatial biases by randomizing the location of the target cards on each trial. She also included no-conflict test cards on half of the trials. These cards matched a target along both dimensions, allowing for an assessment of whether children were actually staying on task.

Results of this study are shown in Figure 16. Children performed quite well on the pre-switch trials and on all no-conflict trials. Critically, when 3-year

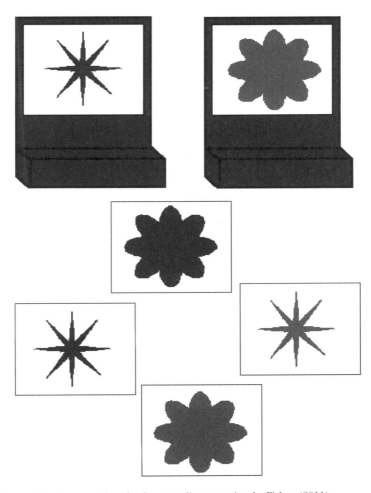

Figure 15.—Cards used in the feature-saliency version by Fisher (2011).

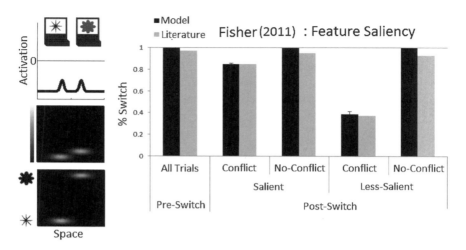

FIGURE 16.—Inputs to the object working memory (WM) model and quantitative fits of the feature-saliency versions in Fisher (2011).

olds had to switch to the salient shape dimension and play the "shape" game, they tended to sort conflict cards correctly. By contrast, when 3-year olds had to switch to the less salient color dimension and play the "color" game, children perseverated on the conflict cards.

Can the DFT capture this pattern of results? To probe this, we gave the model inputs and the task structure taken directly from the methods used by Fisher (2011). We used the same parameters used previously for the 3-year-old model. Figure 16 shows that the simulation results closely follow the pattern of behavior displayed by 3-year olds. In particular, the model showed a high rate of correct sorting for all trials during the pre-switch phase. During the post-switch phase, the model again had a high rate of correct sorting for no-conflict trials with both shape and color rules. Like 3-year olds, however, the model had little difficulty sorting conflict cards by the more salient dimension (e.g., shape), and more difficulty sorting conflict cards by the less-salient dimension (i.e., color).

What is the source of this asymmetry in the model? The asymmetry arises from competition in the color field due to the metrically close target inputs. As seen in the left panel of Figure 16, the target inputs are very close along the color dimension, but are far apart along the shape dimension. Interestingly, this competition is evident even during the pre-switch trials as reflected in the peak-build latency in the shape and color fields. Specifically, the peak-build latency for the pre-switch phase when the model sorted by color was 547 time-steps, while the latency for the pre-switch phase when the model sorted by

66

shape was 425 time-steps. Thus, the model required slightly more time to build a peak in the color field. This difficulty results from the overlap along the feature dimension which leads to competition as the field tries to build peaks at two neighboring color values. That is, extra inhibition is needed to suppress the activation of a nearby task-relevant color. This effect is exacerbated in the post-switch phase when the model tries to sort by color. In this case, the accumulation of Hebbian traces at both spatial locations creates even more conflict. Consequently, the model perseverates and sorts by shape.

Interestingly, we can ask the reverse question: if the 3-year-old model typically perseverates, why does it succeed here when asked to sort by shape during the post-switch trials? Although the behavioral result is the opposite, the explanation is the same: because the colors are metrically close, it is hard for the model to build peaks in the color field due to competition. Consequently, the shape field wins out. Note that the randomization of space actually helps in this case. In contrast to the Standard DCCS task where there is competition in the post-switch field and cooperation in the pre-switch field, here there is competition in both fields going into the post-switch phase.

The PDP of the DCCS (Morton & Munakata, 2002) has addressed the issue of saliency, though through different means. Saliency in the current simulations was instantiated as perceptual similarity; however, saliency in the PDP model was defined by the strength of latent memory traces for preferred or nonpreferred stimuli. In the same way that saliency worked in the current simulations, Morton and Munakata (2002) demonstrated that the PDP model could switch more easily when switching from nonpreferred stimuli with weak latent memory traces.

In summary, the same model and parameters used in our previous simulations quantitatively captures data from Fisher's first experiment. This is nontrivial for the model because spatial locations were randomized. Thus, all effects must come from the metrics of the feature dimensions themselves. In this sense, then, these simulations demonstrate that our account of the development of EF generalizes beyond spatially grounded effects.

Attentional-Weights

Another set of conditions presented in Fisher (2011) manipulated the number of features per dimension. In particular, Fisher compared 3-year olds' ability to switch rules with two versus four features per dimension. This was inspired by work suggesting that attention is a fixed resource (Nosofsky, 1984). Thus, the amount of attention given to a particular object or feature is a function of the total number of features within the scope of attention. As more items are added, less attention is given to each item. Consequently, attention becomes less attached to any particular feature value and can be moved more easily to new features during the post-switch phase.

Fisher (2011) predicted that 3-year olds should show better rule-switching behavior with more items based, once again, on the assumption that automatic, but not voluntary, attention is robust by 3 years. The rationale was as follows. Sorting two features should place a heavy demand on voluntary attention because each item receives more of the attentional resource and, therefore, requires a large voluntary shift of attention to overcome the allocation. Thus, 3-year olds should have difficulty switching rules in this case. Sorting four features, however, should create "lighter" allotments of attention. This should facilitate rule switching because children can rely more on automatic attention.

These predictions were tested in a version of the task comparable to the feature saliency condition. Children were assigned to a condition with either two or four features per dimension (see Figure 17). Eight trials were administered during the pre- and post-switch phases, half of which were no-conflict trials. Again, the spatial locations of the target cards were randomized on each trial. Under these conditions, 3-year-olds had significantly less difficulty switching with four features per dimension than with two features per dimension on conflict trials (see Figure 18).

We examined whether the DNF model could capture these results with the same 3-year-old parameters used previously. Inputs to the model and the

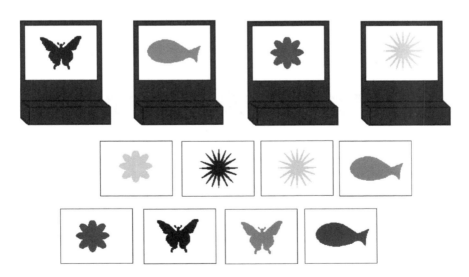

FIGURE 17.—Cards used in the feature-weights version by Fisher (2011).

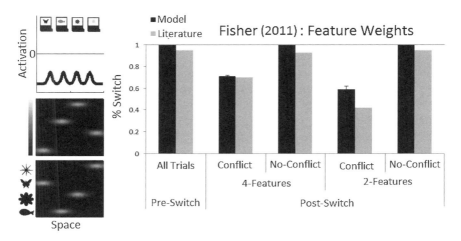

FIGURE 18.—Inputs to the object working memory (WM) model and quantitative fits of the attentional-weights versions in Fisher (2011).

task structure were taken directly from the methods used by Fisher (2011). Figure 18 shows the fit of the model. Once again, the model reproduces the pattern of behavior displayed by 3-year olds. In particular, the model—like children—showed correct sorting for all trials during the pre-switch phase. During the post-switch phase, the model again had a high rate of correct sorting for no-conflict trials with four or two features per dimension. Finally, like 3-year olds, the model had little difficulty sorting conflict cards with four features, and more difficulty with two features (although the model performed better for conflict cards with two features than the children did).

Again, we can probe the source of the asymmetry in performance across conditions. Two factors are important. The first is the fact that individual features are presented less frequently in the four features condition. The second is that the decisions about these features are more spatially distributed since the model is making decisions at four locations instead of two. These factors conspire to produce weaker Hebbian memories in the four-feature condition at the end of the pre-switch phase. In particular, the average strength of Hebbian memories with four features was 0.25 U, while this strength with two features was 0.48 U. Thus, using four features creates weaker memory traces for where the features were sorted in space. Consequently, there is less conflict heading into the post-switch phase due to weaker Hebbian memories overall. This creates less need for inhibition and allows the resting-level modulation to have a stronger influence on the decision-making process. With only two features, Hebbian memories are more concentrated at fewer locations. This creates more conflict and a greater need for inhibition.

Summary of Quantitative Fits Across All Conditions

The simulations in this section demonstrate the versatility of the DNF model, highlighting the role of both feature metrics and the distribution of experience through space and time. These simulations, in conjunction with the previous results, reveal the many factors that influence rule-switching in early childhood. Rule-use between 3 and 5 years is softly assembled "in-the-moment" based on a confluence of factors, including the target and test inputs, memories for features at specific spatial locations, the trial-to-trial dynamics of Hebbian learning, the boosting of attention to particular feature dimensions, and the metric details or number of the stimuli. All of these factors were captured by the DNF model with a single set of parameters at each age.

In total, the current report presented simulation results for 14 different conditions that reflect the model's performance across 57,000 real-time responses. Table 1 shows a summary of all simulated versions. The first column indicates the number of data points simulated for each version. For example, the *Standard 3-year-old* line has two data points corresponding to the pre- and post-switch phases. (Recall that we verified the model showed the correct pattern of pre-switch performance in each case, even though we reported only post-switch performance in the simulation figures). The *2-Features* version, on the other hand, has four data points corresponding to the conflict and no-conflict trials in both the pre- and post-switch phases. The second column lists the number of trials that were included in a single

TABLE 1

SUMMARY OF DATA POINTS AND NUMBER OF TRIALS SIMULATED FOR EACH VERSION OF THE DCCS

Condition	Data Points	Trials	Total Trials
Standard 3-year old	2	12	3,600
Standard 4-year old	2	12	3,600
No-conflict standard	2	12	3,600
Negative priming 3-year old	2	12	3,600
Negative priming 4-year old	2	12	3,600
No-conflict negative priming	2	12	3,600
Partial change	2	12	3,600
Total change	2	12	3,600
Relational complexity	2	12	3,600
Training	3	18	5,400
2-Features	4	16	4,800
4-Features	4	16	4,800
To-salient	4	16	4,800
To-less-salient	4	16	4,800
Total	**37**	**190**	**57,000**

simulation of each version. Finally, the third column indicates the total number of trials across all simulations for each version.

To evaluate the model's performance across the 37 data points we quantitatively fit, we computed the root mean squared error (RMSE) between the simulated and empirical data. The overall RMSE was very good at 0.06. Thus, the model results were typically within 6% of the empirical values—an impressive result, particularly given that we used the same parameters across all variants of the DCCS task.

VII. GENERAL DISCUSSION

Executive function is an important aspect of cognition because control and regulation are central in numerous cognitive domains. It is an especially important topic of study in early childhood because it is during this period that EF begins to emerge and undergo dramatic and lasting changes. Moreover, measures of EF during early childhood robustly predict physical health, substance dependence, personal finances, and criminal offending outcomes nearly three decades later (Moffitt et al., 2011). Further, preschool interventions aimed at improving EF have produced significant increases in school achievement and behavioral function (Diamond & Lee, 2011). Thus, EF is a central aspect of cognition that undergoes foundational changes in early childhood.

The goal of the present work was to take a first step toward a new theory of the development of EF using the DCCS task as a case study. The DNF model presented here moves beyond previous theories of the DCCS by integrating the processes of object WM and dimensional attention to construct a neurally grounded model of rule use. Critically, we were able to quantitatively capture a wide range of effects in the literature, focusing on a key transition in EF between 3 and 5 years. Further, we generated a novel set of predictions from the model that no other theory readily explains. In the sections that follow, we situate DFT in the context of current theories of the DCCS task as well as the broader literature on EF. We then discuss limitations of the theory and the important challenges that lie ahead as we pursue a theory of autonomous development and ties between DFT and the growing literature on the neural bases of EF.

Comparing the DFT to Other Theories

The DFT of the DCCS shares many similarities with current theories of the DCCS. Both CCC/CCC-r theory and the PDP model suggest that rule-use and EF are emergent phenomena of a complex system. Likewise, rule-use in the DNF model emerged from neural interactions within and across multiple cortical fields. Our DNF model also implements a common conceptualization of how inhibitory and working memory processes relate—specifically, inhibitory processes in the DNF are a result of activating a working memory representation (see Marcovitch & Zelazo, 1999; Morton & Munakata, 2002; Stedron et al., 2005; see also Roberts & Pennington, 1996; Roberts et al., 1994). Further, CCC/CCC-r theory explains flexible rule-use as the product of linguistically guided reflection on the task rules. The DNF model provides a bridge to this view by using dimensional labels as the basis for selective attention. In this respect, our model is also similar to the PDP model which posits that "color" and "shape" representations in frontal cortex guide attention to dimensions in the DCCS task. Finally, our developmental account is similar to the account proposed by Morton and Munakata (2002). They increased the strength of recurrent interactions in the PDP model, boosting the active representation of rules in a bank of PFC nodes. Stronger neural interactions in our dimensional attention system achieved a similar effect.

Although the DNF model shares similarities with existing accounts, there are also critical differences. One key difference between the DNF model and CCC/CCCr theory is that our theory is not strictly hierarchical. Although the dimensional attention system can be characterized as a "top-down" rule representation, rules in the DNF model are distributed across multiple reciprocally coupled neural systems. For instance, the dimensional attention system does not "know" all the details of the rules; rather, this system creates a bias, but then off-loads the detailed decision-making to the feature WM fields. Similarly, the feature fields "know" the details of the specific stimulus-response mappings, but these fields do not "know" the higher order goals of the task (e.g., sort by shape or color). This type of distributed neural organization can enable flexible behavior and the "soft assembly" of rule-like behavior, that is, success or failure can come from multiple sources. For instance, the DNF model was able to explain effects that arise from manipulations to the attentional saliency of the features across dimensions (Fisher, 2011; see also Honomichl & Chen, 2011). CCC/CCC-r theory does not explain how the featural properties of the objects influence the representation of a rule hierarchy or the ability to consciously reflect on the rule-structure.

Regarding the PDP model, the key difference is that the DNF model binds features together into integrated objects, while the PDP model is uni-dimensional—it does not learn about the unattended feature values as it "sorts" cards. Thus, when the connectionist model sorts a red circle to a red star during the pre-switch phase, it forms no memory for the circle feature. Rather, latent traces are strengthened only along the dimension used for sorting on each trial. Critically, our quantitative simulations show that learning along the irrelevant dimension plays an important role in several variants of the DCCS task. For example, in the No-Conflict version, the overlap of Hebbian memories and target inputs during the pre-switch phase for the irrelevant dimension provided a sufficient boost when these features became relevant during the post-switch phase. This allowed the model to correctly switch rules (for related results, see the No-Conflict Negative Priming version). It is unclear how the connectionist model would explain children's successful performance in this condition. Further, in the Negative Priming version, the conflict between Hebbian memories and target inputs along the irrelevant feature dimension was critical for simulating children's failure in this version of the task. Here, it is unclear how the connectionist model would capture these findings because latent traces during the pre-switch phase would only be strengthened for the specific pre-switch feature values. Once these values are changed during the post-switch phase, the model would not have a bias to continue sorting by the pre-switch dimension.

Another difference relative to the PDP model is in our account of development. We proposed that there is a refinement of the pattern of connectivity between the frontal nodes and posterior cortical fields over development in addition to changes in recurrent activation which are common to both models (see Morton & Munakata, 2002). Future work will be needed to determine whether this difference across accounts is an "in kind" difference or simply a difference in emphasis that could be incorporated into both accounts.

More generally, the DFT is unique among all accounts in the special role space plays in the binding of features and the spatially grounded learning across trials. This feature of the model was central to the novel predictions we successfully tested in the present report. Moreover, our simulation results suggest that spatial conflict or cooperation within feature fields plays an important role in many different variants of the DCCS task. Finally, it is worth noting that although our model differs from previous accounts in many respects, the DFT was still able to account for key findings central to other theories of the DCCS. For example, the model simulated the results from versions in which the features were changed between the pre- and post-switch phases (e.g., Negative Priming, Partial Change, or Total Change), which were critical results for CCC/CCC-r theory. The DNF model was also able to capture the improvement in switching that results from training before the post-switch phase, as predicted by the PDP model (Brace et al., 2006).

DFT and Executive Function

Although we focused on the DCCS task in the simulations reported here, our findings provide a critical step toward a general theory of the development of EF. In particular, unlike previous conceptual theories of the DCCS, the DFT can address the multicomponent nature of EF. Critically, DFT demonstrates how these components can emerge from system-wide interactions in the neural architecture. For instance, building a WM peak in a feature field can actively inhibit the prepotent response associated with a previously relevant feature value. Moreover, the formation of a WM peak can be biased by the boost provided by a dimensional attention node as the system attempts to switch rules. Thus, all three processes conspire together to enable flexible behavior and to explain the myriad findings in the literature. Within the DFT framework, the functional aspects of "inhibitory control," "working memory," and "switching" all emerged from general neural dynamics around the input structure of particular tasks.

Other work highlights how these processes in the DNF model offer a robust framework for thinking about executive function more generally. For example, Thelen et al. (2001) simulated the early development of inhibitory control in the A-not-B task using the concepts of dynamic field theory. In this case, successful reaches to the B location were driven by a peak of activation at the B location that persisted over the delay after the cue to reach to the B location. Relatedly, Spencer, Simmering, and coworkers (Simmering, 2008; Simmering et al., 2008) have used a layered dynamic field architecture to simulate critical aspects of working memory and change detection performance, including increases in working memory capacity over development. Changes in capacity resulted from increases in the strength of local-excitation and lateral inhibition—the same developmental mechanism probed here (Simmering, 2008). DFT has also provided a theoretical framework for another aspect of EF—response selection. For instance, Erlhagen and Schöner (2002) captured the Simon effect through competitive inhibitory dynamics associated with the imperative stimulus and the spatial location of a stimulus. And current work is trying to integrate aspects of these specific models with the work presented here. For instance, we are currently using the EF model presented here to capture canonical response inhibition tasks (Simon, Go/No-Go), WM tasks (change detection), and tasks that tap task-switching or task-coordination (DCCS, dual-task). The large goal of this work is to understand how an integrated neural process model can give rise to behavioral signatures of performance across these different tasks, including the latent factor structure evident in studies of individual differences (Lehto et al., 2003; Miyake et al., 2000).

Beyond these efforts, we are also working to generalize the concepts of DFT beyond the laboratory into real-world EF. Sandamirskaya and Schöner (2010) used DFT to explore how an autonomous robotic system might organize its behaviors in a real-world context in real time. Autonomous robotics offers an exciting platform for probing the details of EF because behavioral organization in the real-world creates novel challenges that are typically not present in laboratory tasks. For instance, in the DCCS task, the rule-switch is specified by the experimenter. But oftentimes, rule-switches must be internally and autonomously generated. This requires that one determine whether the current goal has been achieved by, for instance, perceiving that the correct state of affairs has been created in the world. Next, the current goal must be deactivated, and the new goal state must be brought into an active neural state.

Sandamirskaya and Schöner (2010) showed that an autonomous robot using DFT could actively organize its behavior in time. In one demonstration, a robot was taught a sequence of colors. The robot was then allowed to freely navigate in a playpen with an array of colored blocks. The task was to find the blocks in the correct sequence. This is a challenging robotics task because the robot must keep the current goal state actively in mind (e.g., find the green object) as it navigates around the playpen. Once it detects green, it must then navigate successfully to the object, avoiding obstacles along the way. When it arrives at the green block, the color green dominates the camera image. This was the "condition of satisfaction" used by the robot to destabilize the "green" goal and bring up the next goal in the sequence. The robotic architecture used by Sandamirskaya and Schöner effectively learned a color sequence and autonomously organized its behavior in the playpen to find the blocks in the correct sequence. Importantly, the details of the robot's behavior were not pre-programmed; rather, the robot behaved in real time based on its own, autonomously generated neural dynamics. Note, further, that details of the robot's neural architecture had several similarities with the DNF model proposed in the present report. Most critically, the robotic model modulated its own behavior through time by boosting cortical fields tuned to specific features—the same neural mechanism implemented here.

Neural Basis of EF and Rule-Use

A critical strength of DFT is the ability to explicitly tie the dynamics of the model to neural function. DFT operates based on general properties of neural activation distributed across cortical layers (Douglas & Martin, 1998), and the local-excitatory/laterally inhibitory interactions that arise from such interactions. These interactions give rise to stable neural patterns (Durstewitz, Seamans, & Sejnowski, 2000) that form the basis of thinking and decision-making in DFT. Critically, these neural dynamics have been shown to be robustly linked to single- and multi-unit recordings in both visual and motor cortex (Bastian et al., 1998, 2003; Erlhagen et al., 1999; Jancke et al., 1999), as well as to neural population dynamics measured using voltage-sensitive dye imaging (Markounikau et al., 2010).

An important next step for DFT is to link to neural measures from human cognitive tasks. An initial step has been taken in this direction by linking DFT to ERP measures in the context of movement planning and multi-object tracking (McDowell et al., 2002; Spencer, Barich et al., 2012). We have also been developing an approach that links DFT to the BOLD signal recorded with fMRI based on biophysical work that suggests that such a mapping is possible (Deco & Rolls, 2004; Logothetis et al., 2001). In this approach, we record a real-time neural signal analogous to a local field potential from each cortical field in our model. We can then use this real-time neural signal to generate hemodynamic responses directly from the model. These can then be analyzed using the same tools used in fMRI research. The question is whether the simulated hemodynamics from the model quantitatively match hemodynamic data measured with fMRI.

This can achieve multiple goals. First, we can ask whether the neural dynamics within different fields in the model reflect the localized neural dynamics measured with fMRI. When we introduced the model in Chapter III, we made several localization assumptions based on the extant fMRI literature, but it will be important for future work to probe these localization assumptions directly. Second, efforts to map from simulated neural field activity to fMRI can constrain modeling efforts, asking whether we can simultaneously capture both behavioral and neural dynamics (Ashby & Waldschmidt, 2008). It is possible, for instance, that multiple collections of model parameters can capture relevant behavioral data, but only a small subset of parameters can capture both behavioral *and* fMRI data. Third, if the mapping between the DNF model and fMRI is robust, we can test the DNF model by generating not only behavioral predictions, but also *neural predictions* based on how activation evolves over time as the model, for instance, sorts cards in variants of the DCCS task.

This could be particularly useful in the case of EF given the complexity of the frontal systems involved in cognitive flexibility. For instance, model-based approaches to fMRI might help unpack the frontal system in our current architecture by isolating different functional components that are associated with activity in different frontal regions. In this way, we can use fMRI to go beyond simply asking *where* a cognitive function is localized to address *how* neural activity is functionally related to cognition (Ashby & Waldschmidt, 2008). This is a critical step in probing the neural mechanisms underlying EF.

We have taken a first step in this direction by using a dynamic field architecture similar to the one reported here to capture aspects of dual-task performance including changes in behavioral (reaction times) and fMRI data over learning (Buss et al., 2014). The dual-task model has posterior neural populations that associate visual or auditory stimuli with manual or vocal responses. These two-dimensional neural fields are coupled to a dimensional attention system that modulates the resting level of the posterior fields when a stimulus is presented.

We used this model to capture a behavioral and neural dataset reported by Dux et al. (2009). This study exposed participants to dual- and single-task conditions over 8 days of practice with fMRI conducted at the beginning, middle, and end of training. These researchers identified a region in inferior frontal cortex that closely followed dual-task costs over practice. That is, early in learning, inferior frontal cortex showed a large response that reduced to single-task levels by the end of practice. The model showed these same neural signatures due to Hebbian learning in both the modality-specific, posterior fields and the dimensional attention system (see Buss et al., 2014). Most critically, after exposing the model to the training regimen used by Dux et al. (2009), we found that changes in the hemodynamic response generated from the dimensional attention system closely paralleled changes in inferior frontal cortex activation over learning. And the same model produced reaction times that quantitatively matched the empirical data from both single and dual-task conditions over learning.

Work in our laboratory has also examined the developmental changes in frontal activation in the DCCS task reported by Moriguchi and Hiraki (2009). Initial simulations using our approach to generating hemodynamics from the DNF model show that the autonomous dimensional attention system reported in Chapter III can qualitatively reproduce the frontal activation differences from Moriguchi and Hiraki (see Spencer & Buss, under review). This opens up exciting possibilities to probe specific hemodynamic predictions *over development* using our EF model (see Spencer & Buss, under review).

Limitations of the DFT and Future Directions

In the present report, we used DFT to show how an autonomous dimensional attention system coupled to an object WM model could capture children's performance in the standard DCCS task. Nevertheless, when we simulated children's performance in quantitative detail, we simplified the dimensional attention system by using distributions of *boost* and *shift* parameters for each age group. This allowed us to probe whether specific developmental changes to the dimensional attention system were sufficient to capture children's performance. A critical next step in theory development, therefore, is to probe whether we can capture developmental changes in EF within a fully autonomous neural system.

In principle, each developmental change implemented by hand in our model could emerge from a Hebbian learning process. The first developmental change we implemented increased the strength of excitatory and inhibitory neural interactions within the dimensional attention system. It is likely that this modification can emerge from the same Hebbian process already incorporated in the DNF model if the model's behavior were simulated across many, many trials. In particular, as the model repeatedly activates the "color" or "shape" node, this will increase the strength of the Hebbian trace for a particular node. Stronger excitation can, in turn, lead to an effective strengthening of inhibitory interactions as the nodes competitively interact. Indeed, these types of changes were evident in our simulations of the dual-task model, which autonomously learned to organize its behavior over practice (Buss et al., 2014).

The second developmental change we implemented by hand refined the pattern of connectivity between the frontal and posterior systems. Again, in principle, this can be tackled with a Hebbian process that learns the patterns of covariance between, for instance, activation of a "color" node and activation patterns in the color WM field (see, e.g., Sandamirskaya & Schöner, 2010). But this points toward another critical piece of the developmental puzzle. Conceptually in the model, the dimensional nodes represent a mapping between a neural population representation in frontal cortex and cortical fields in posterior brain regions tuned to different feature dimensions. Left out of our developmental account, at present, is that fact that children are, in reality, learning something specific about dimensional attention as they learn dimensional labels in early word learning (e.g., Sandhofer & Smith, 1999, 2001). This highlights the need to link our theory to the literature on early word learning, which will require consideration of the learning opportunities that children have and the developmental time course of dimensional label learning. Although challenging, linking to this literature will undoubtedly provide robust constraints for theory development as we attempt to integrate findings from multiple paradigms across different domains of cognitive development.

Note that related work with DFT has already moved in this direction. Specifically, Faubel and Schöner (2008) implemented fast word learning using dynamic neural fields in an autonomous, interactive robot. In their work, the perceptual features of objects were bound together along a label dimension similar to how features are bound through space in the model presented here. Using relatively few training trials, the robot was able to form categories of objects using the graded associations between features and labels, which facilitated accurate recognition of an assortment of real-world items. This work demonstrates that an associative mechanism within dynamic neural fields can serve as a basis for functionally linking labels and feature fields. And, critically, labels in this context need not be associated with specific features; rather, labels such as "shape" and "color" can be associated with entire feature dimensions (for related work in early word learning with children, see Samuelson, Schutte, & Horst, 2009; Samuelson et al., 2011). In summary, then, although our theory, at present, lacks an autonomous account of development, we contend that this key goal is within reach.

Finally, we note that there are variations of the DCCS task that require model modification to effectively capture findings from the literature. For instance, Kloo and Perner (2005) showed that separating the dimensions on the test cards improved rule switching with 3-year-olds (see Figure 1H), but separating the dimensions on the target cards had no such effect. To examine whether we could capture this version with the DNF model, we first separated the features on the target cards. This resulted in high levels of perseveration in the model (75% perseveration), comparable to empirical findings (see Kloo

& Perner, 2005). This decomposition of features at separate spatial locations has little impact because the posterior fields still have the canonical layout of cooperation or competition across fields, now just distributed across four total locations instead of two.

But what about separating the features on the test cards? Here we must consider how visual attention might be modulated by this manipulation. Recall that the test card inputs come into the posterior fields as ridges. Conceptually, this reflects input from early visual areas as the model attends to the features on the test card (see, e.g., Spencer, Austin, et al., 2012). With the features separated in the space of the test card, it is possible that children might spatially attend slightly more to the task-relevant features, producing an imbalance in the strength of inputs for the different dimensions (see, Harrison & Tong, 2009). To examine this hypothesis with the model, we applied the *shift* and *boost* parameters to the strength of ridge inputs for the test cards. With this manipulation, the model now showed a high rate of switching (80% rate of switching) similar to the effect reported in the literature (Diamond et al., 2005; Kloo & Perner, 2005; Zelazo et al., 2003). Thus, these results are within reach with a modest change to the model implementation.

Other results are more clearly beyond what the current model architecture is capable of simulating. Some of these would require a more extensive autonomous dimensional attention system. For example, Yerys and Muankata (2006) showed that different manipulations to the labels for the games or the features used in a task can make switching easier for 3-year-olds. This effect may be within reach as we pursue links between the emergence of EF in development and how children use words for the different "games" they play in the DCCS task.

Similarly, CCC explains changes in flexible rule-use through conscious reflection rather than the real-time dynamics of representing and using a set of rules. For example, one study that has been used to support CCC/CCC-r theory instructed children to wait and think about the rules before the start of the post-switch phase (Deák et al., 2004). In this case, performance significantly improved when children were given this additional opportunity for reflection. Although conscious reflection has no explicit role in the DNF, it too could be depicted as an emergent outcome of the ability to robustly and selectively activate a dimensional label. For example, if we were to de-boost the object representation system to prevent it from making a decision, this would allow the dimensional attention system to accumulate more activation from the rule input. In the autonomous version of our model, this could result in enhanced performance for the "young" model.

In another version, 4- and 5-year-old children were given no-conflict cards at the beginning of the post-switch phase. These children—who would typically be able to switch rules—made more errors in the post-switch phase with an increasing number of no-conflict trials (Marcovitch, Boseovski, & Knapp, 2007). The authors termed this goal-neglect. When the need to maintain a goal is no longer needed (as in the case with no-conflict cards), focus becomes relaxed and the goal can ultimately be neglected once it needs to be used again (on a conflict trial). In principle, such an effect could stem from the reciprocal coupling between the feature WM fields and the dimensional attention system. For instance, we might modify the dimensional attention system such that it is only engaged when conflict must be resolved (for related ideas, see Botvinick, Braver, Barch, Carter, & Cohen, 2001). In this context, a series of no-conflict trials could slow down subsequent build-up of activation of the dimensional attention system.

One further version that challenges our model showed that 3-year-olds perseverate even after only a single pre-switch trial (Zelazo et al., 1996). This is also the case with many model simulations; however, 70% of the simulations showed an intermediate pattern of switching where three out of the six post-switch cards were sorted incorrectly. The model only received one test during the pre-switch phase and, thus, only established Hebbian memories for those features. During the post-switch, then, the models tended to incorrectly sort the card it received in the pre-switch while correctly sorting the card it did not receive during the pre-switch phase. Thus, although these simulation results match the empirical findings once we drop intermediate responding (see Zelazo et al., 1996), the simulated data do not match the fact that only 8% of children showed intermediate responses during the post-switch trials. The majority of models (>75%), however, perseverate in this version when we implement demonstrations of the pre-switch rules as in the standard procedure (Zelazo et al., 2003, 1996). Demonstrations were not administered in the simulations we presented in previous chapters to simplify the implementation of the task. With demonstrations in this version, though, Hebbian memories are established for both conjunctions of features on the test cards leading to perseveration along both test cards. These simulation results point to a possible role of pre-switch demonstrations in perseveration, which has not previously been explored in the literature. We will probe this in future work as we implement a more expansive autonomous dimensional attention system.

CONCLUSION

The theory we presented here shows promise in its ability to integrate the multiple processes of EF. These emerged from interactive neural dynamics across multiple cortical fields and the details of the DCCS tasks we simulated. The DFT was able to quantitatively capture a wide array of empirical results from a canonical task used to examine the early development of EF.

Moreover, this theory generated a set of novel predictions that we successfully tested here. In this context, DFT offers the most comprehensive account of children's performance in the DCCS task to date and provides a robust starting point for a theory of the development of executive function.

EF undergoes critical changes in early childhood that have lasting effects later in life, predicting academic achievement and life-time satisfaction. What are the implications of our work for this literature? As we sketched above, we are moving from simple tasks like the DCCS that are ideal for use in early development to the array of tasks used with older children and adults. As we do this, it will be important to connect up with the complex neural literature on this topic. In this regard, efforts to map activation dynamics in DNF models to ERPs and fMRI offer an innovative approach to link our theory to neural data. In addition, we are moving from laboratory tasks to real-world contexts in collaboration with our colleagues using autonomous robotics to get a better understanding of EF "in the wild." Together, this work will paint a broad picture of how EF is organized across tasks, across the levels of brain and behavior, across development, and across contexts.

Moreover, DFT presents the opportunity to bridge to intervention settings in a way that can speak to both cognitive and neural development. For instance, one possibility is that we could capture the performance of both typically and atypically developing individuals to simulate individual developmental trajectories (for discussion, see Perone, in press). We could then try out specific interventions with the model and predict which types of intervention might be most useful. There is precedent for this type of an approach in the literature. For instance, models have played an instrumental role in several studies examining the processes that underlie dyslexia (Harm & Seidenburg, 1999; Plaut, McClelland, Seidenberg, & Patterson, 1996) and specific language impairment (Joanisse & Seidenberg, 2003; McMurray, Samelson, Lee, & Tomblin, 2010). Although formalizing such an approach to intervention work is in its infancy, this would constitute an exciting opportunity to not just use computational models as tools for understanding and integrating findings in the literature, but for moving beyond what is known to predict what might matter in the real world.

REFERENCES

Aggelopoulos, N. C., & Rolls, E. T. (2005). Scene perception: Inferior temporal cortex neurons encode the positions of different objects in the scene. *European Journal of Neuroscience*, **22**, 2903–2916.

Amari, S. (1977). Dynamics of pattern formation in lateral-inhibition type neural fields. *Biological Cybernetics*, **27**, 77–87.

Amari, S. (1980). Topographic organization of nerve fields. *Bulletin of Mathematical Biology*, **42**, 339–364.

Amari, S., & Arbib, M. A. (1977). Competition and cooperation in neural nets. In J. Metzler (Ed.), *Systems neuroscience* (pp. 119–165). New York: Academic Press.

Andersen, R. A. (1995). Encoding of intention and spatial location in the posterior parietal cortex. *Cerebral Cortex*, **5**, 457–469.

Anderson, J. R. (1993). *Rules of the mind*. Hillsdale, NJ: Lawrence Erlbaum.

Ashby, F. G., & Waldschmidt, J. G. (2008). Fitting computational models to fMRI data. *Behavior Research Methods*, **40**(3), 713–721.

Asaad, W. F., Rainer, G., & Miller, E. K. (2000). Task-specific neural activity in the primate prefrontal cortex. *The Journal of Neurophysiology*, **84**(1), 451–459.

Baddeley, A. D. (1986). *Working memory*. Oxford: Clarendon Press.

Baddeley, A. D., Della Sala, S., Papagno, C., & Spinnler, H. (1997). Dual-task performance in dysexecutive and nondysexecutive patients with a frontal lesion. *Neuropsychology*, **11**, 187–194.

Baird, A. A., Kagan, J., Gaudette, T., Walz, K. A., Hershlag, N., & Boas, D. A. (2002). Frontal lobe activation during object permanence: Data from near-infrared spectroscopy. *NeuroImage*, **16**(4), 1120–1126.

Barnea-Goraly, N., Menon, V., Eckert, M., Tamm, L., Bammer, R., Karchemskiy, A., Dant, C. C., & Reiss, A. L. (2005). White matter development during childhood and adolescence: A cross-sectional diffusion tensor imaging study. *Cerebral Cortex*, **15**(12), 1848–1854.

Bastian, A., Riehle, A., Erlhagen, W., & Schöner, G. (1998). Prior information preshapes the population representation of movement direction in motor cortex. *Neuroreport*, **9**, 315–319.

Bastian, A., Schöner, G., & Riehle, A. (2003). Preshaping and continuous evolution of motor cortical representations during movement preparation. *European Journal of Neuroscience*, **18**, 2047–2058.

Behrens, T. E. J., Woolrich, M. W., Walton, M. W., & Rushworth, M. F. S. (2007). Learning the value of information in an uncertain world. *Nature Neuroscience*, **10**, 1214–1221.

Biederman, J., Petty, C. R., Fried, R., Doyle, A. E., Spencer, T., Seidman, L. J., Gross, L., Poetzl, K., & Faraone, S. V. (2007). Stability of executive function deficits into young adult years: A prospective longitudinal follow-up study of grown up males with ADHD. *Acta Psychiatrica Scandivica*, **116**, 129–136.

Blair, C. B., & Razza, R. P. (2007). Relating effortful control, executive function, and false belief understanding to emerging math and literacy ability in kindergarten. *Child Development,* **78**(2), 647–663.

Bohlman, N. L., & Fenson, L. (2005). The effects of feedback on children's perseverative errors. *Journal of Cognition and Development,* **6**(1), 119–131.

Botvinick, M. M., Braver, T. S., Barch, D. M., Carter, C. S., & Cohen, J. D. (2001). Conflict monitoring and cognitive control. *Psychological Review,* **108**(3), 624–652.

Brace, J. J., Morton, J. B., & Munakata, Y. (2006). When actions speak louder than words: Improving children's flexibility in a card-sorting task. *Psychological Science,* **17**(8), 665–669.

Brooks, P. J., Hanauer, J. B., Padowska, B., & Rosman, H. (2003). The role of selective attention in preschoolers' rule use in a novel dimensional card sort. *Cognitive Development,* **18**, 195–215.

Bull, R., & Scerif, G. (2001). Executive function as a predictor of children's mathematical ability: Inhibition, switching, and working memory. *Developmental Neuropsychology,* **19**(3), 273–293.

Bunge, S. A. (2004). How we use rules to select actions: A review of evidence from cognitive neuroscience. *Cognitive, Affective, & Behavioral Neuroscience,* **4**(4), 564–579.

Bunge, S. A., Wallis, J. D., Parker, A., Brass, M., Crone, E. A., Hoshi, E., & Sakai, K. (2005). Neural circuitry underlying rule use in humans and nonhuman primates. *The Journal of Neuroscience,* **9**, 10347–10350.

Bunge, S. A., & Zelazo, P. D. (2006). A brain-based account of the development of rule use in childhood. *Current Directions in Psychological Science,* **15**(3), 118–121.

Buss, A. T., Wifall, T., Hazeltine, E., & Spencer, J. P. (2014). Integrating the behavioral and neural dynamics of response selection in a dual-task paradigm: A dynamic field model of Dux et al. (2009). *Journal of Cognitive Neuroscience,* **26**, 334–351.

Carlson, S. M. (2005). Developmentally sensitive measures of executive function in preschool children. *Developmental Neuropsychology,* **28**(2), 595–616.

Carlson, S. M., Moses, L. J., & Breton, C. (2002). How specific is the relation between executive function and theory of mind? Contributions of inhibitory control and working memory. *Infant and Child Development,* **11**, 73–92.

Clearfield, M. W., Dineva, E., Smith, L. B., Diedrich, F. J., & Thelen, E. (2009). Cue salience and infant perseverative reaching: Tests of the dynamic field theory. *Developmental Science,* **12**(1), 26–40.

Collette, F., Van der Linden, M., Laureys, S., Delfiore, G., Degueldre, C., Luxen, A., & Salmon, E. (2005). Exploring the unity and diversity of the neural substrates of executive functioning. *Human Brain Mapping,* **25**(4), 409–423.

Compte, A., Brunel, N., Goldman-Rakic, P. S., & Wang, X.-J. (2000). Synaptic mechanisms and network dynamics underlying spatial working memory in a cortical network model. *Cerebral Cortex,* **10**, 910–923.

Corbett, B. A., Constantine, L. J., Hendren, R., Rocke, D., & Ozonoff, S. (2009). Examining executive functioning in children with autism spectrum disorder, attention deficit hyperactivity disorder and typical development. *Psychiatry Research,* **166**(2–3), 210–222.

Courtney, S. M. (2004). Attention and cognitive control as emergent properties of information representation in working memory. *Cognitive, Affective, & Behavioral Neuroscience,* **4**(4), 501–516.

Cowan, N., Elliott, E. M., Saults, J. S., Morey, C. C., Mattox, S., Hismjatullina, A., & Conway, A. R. A. (2005). On the capacity of attention: Its estimation and its role in working memory and cognitive aptitudes. *Cognitive Psychology*, **51**(1), 42–100.

Cragg, L., & Nation, K. (2008). Go or no-go? Developmental improvements in the efficiency of response inhibition in mid-childhood. *Developmental Science*, **11**(6), 819–827.

Crone, E. A., Donohue, S. E., Honomichl, R., Wendelken, C., & Bunge, S. A. (2006). Brain regions mediating flexible rule use during development. *The Journal of Neuroscience*, **26**(43), 11239–11247.

Crone, E. A., Wendelken, C., Donohue, S. E., & Bunge, S. A. (2006). Neural evidence for dissociable components of task-switching. *Cerebral Cortex*, **16**, 475–486.

Crone, E. A., Wendelken, C., Donohue, S. E., van Leijenhorst, L., & Bunge, S. A. (2006). Neurocognitive development of the ability to manipulate information in working memory. *Proceedings of the National Academy of Sciences*, **103**(24), 9315–9320.

Cui, X., Bray, S., Bryant, D. M., Glover, G. H., & Reiss, A. L. (2011). A quantitative comparison of NIRS and fMRI across multiple cognitive tasks. *NeuroImage*, **54**(4), 2808–2821.

Davidson, N. C., Amso, D., Anderson, L. C., & Diamond, A. (2006). Development of cognitive control and executive functions from 4 to 13 years: Evidence from manipulations of memory, inhibition, and task switching. *Neuropsychologia*, **44**(11), 2037–2078.

Deák, G. O., Ray, S. D., & Pick, A. D. (2004). Effects of age, reminders, and task-difficulty on young children's rule-switching flexibility. *Cognitive Development*, **19**, 385–400.

Deco, G., & Rolls, E. T. (2004). A neurodynamical cortical model of visual attention and invariant object recognition. *Vision Research*, **44**(6), 621–642.

Deco, G., & Rolls, E. T. (2005). Attention, short-term memory, and action selection: A unifying theory. *Progress in Neurobiology*, **76**, 236–256.

Dempster, F. N. (1981). Memory span: Sources of individual and developmental differences. *Psychological Bulletin*, **89**(1), 63–100.

Dempster, F. N. (1992). The rise and fall of the inhibitory mechanism: Toward a unified theory of cognitive development and aging. *Developmental Review*, **12**(1), 45–75.

Desimone, R., & Gross, C. G. (1979). Visual areas in the temporal cortex of the macaque. *Brain Research*, **178**(2–3), 363–380.

Diamond, A. (2002). Normal development of prefrontal cortex from birth to young adulthood: Cognitive functions, anatomy, and biochemistry. In D. T. Stuss & R. T. Knight (Eds.), *Principles of frontal lobe function* (pp. 406–503). Oxford: Oxford University Press.

Diamond, A., Carlson, S. M., & Beck, D. M. (2005). Preschool children's performance in task switching on the dimensional change card sort task: Separating the dimensions aids the ability to switch. *Developmental Neuropsychology*, **28**(2), 689–729.

Diamond, A., & Kirkham, N. Z. (2005). Not quite as grown up as we like to think: Parallels between cognition in childhood adulthood. *Psychological Science*, **16**(4), 291–297.

Diamond, A., & Lee, K. (2011). Interventions shown to aid executive function development in children 4 to 12 years old. *Science*, **333**, 959–964.

DiCarlo, J. J., & Maunsell, J. H. (2003). Anterior inferotemporal neurons of monkeys engaged in object recognition can be highly sensitive to object retinal position. *Journal of Neurophysiology*, **89**, 3264–3278.

Dosenbach, N. U. F., Fair, D. A., Miezin, F. M., Cohen, A. L., Wenger, K. K., Dosenbach, R. A. T., Fox, M. D., Snyder, A. Z., Vincent, J. L., Raichle, M. E., Schlagger, B. L., & Petersen, S. E.

(2007). Distinct brain networks for adaptive and stable task control in humans. *Proceedings of the National Academy of Sciences*, **104**(26), 11073–11078.

Douglas, R., & Martin, K. (1998). Neocortex. In G. M. Shepherd (Ed.), *The synaptic organization of the brain* (pp. 459–509). New York: Oxford University Press.

Dowsett, S. M., & Livesey, D. J. (2000). The development of inhibitory control in preschool children: Effects of "executive skills" training. *Developmental Psychobiology*, **36**(2), 161–174.

Drucker, D. M., & Aguirre, G. K. (2009). Different spatial scales of shape similarity representation in lateral and ventral LOC. *Cerebral Cortex*, **19**, 2269–2280.

Duncan, J., Emslie, H., Williams, P., Johnson, R., & Freer, C. (1996). Intelligence and the frontal lobe: The organization of goal-directed behavior. *Cognitive Psychology*, **30**, 257–303.

Duncan, J., Johnson, R., Swales, M., & Freer, C. (1997). Frontal lobe deficits after head injury: Unity and diversity of function. *Cognitive Neuropsychology*, **14**(5), 713–741.

Dunn, J. R. (2010). Health behavior vs the stress of low socioeconomic status and health outcomes. *Journal of the American Medical Association*, **303**(12), 1199–1200.

Durstewitz, D., Seamans, J. K., & Sejnowski, T. J. (2000). Neurocomputational models of working memory. *Nature Neuroscience Supplement*, **3**, 1184–1191.

Durston, S., Thomas, K. M., Yang, Y., Ulug, A. M., Zimmerman, R. D., & Casey, B. J. (2002). A neural basis for the development of inhibitory control. *Developmental Science*, **5**(4), F9–F16.

Dux, P. E., Tombu, M. N., Harrison, S., Rogers, B. P., Tong, F., & Marois, R. (2009). Training improves multitasking performance by increasing the speed of information processing in human prefrontal cortex. *Neuron*, **63**(1), 127–138.

Eakin, L., Minde, K., Hechtman, L., Ochs, E., Krane, E., Bouffard, R., Greenfield, B., & Looper, K. (2004). The marital and family functioning of adults with ADHD and their spouses. *Journal of Attentional Disorder*, **8**(1), 1–10.

Edin, F., Klingberg, T., Johansson, P., McNab, F., Tegnér, J., & Compte, A. (2009). Mechanism for top-down control of working memory capacity. *Proceedings of the National Academy of Sciences*, **106**, 6802–6807.

Edin, F., Macoveanu, J., Olesen, P., Tegnér, J., & Klingberg, T. (2007). Stronger synaptic connectivity as a mechanism behind development of working-memory related brain activity during childhood. *Journal of Cognitive Neuroscience*, **19**(5), 750–760.

Egner, T., & Hirsch, J. (2005). Cognitive control mechanisms resolve conflict through cortical amplification of task-relevant information. *Nature Neuroscience*, **8**(12), 1784–1790.

Erlhagen, W., Bastian, A., Jancke, D., Riehle, A., & Schöner, G. (1999). The distribution of neuronal population activation (DPA) as a tool to study interaction and integration of cortical representations. *Journal of Neuroscience Methods*, **94**, 53–66.

Erlhagen, W., & Schöner, G. (2002). Dynamic field theory of movement preparation. *Psychological Review*, **109**(3), 545–572.

Fair, D. A., Cohen, A. L., Dosenbach, N. U. F., Church, J. A., Miezin, F. M., Barch, D. M., Raichle, M. E., Petersen, S. E., & Schlaggar, B. L. (2008). The maturing architecture of the brain's default network. *Proceedings of the National Academy of Sciences*, **105**, 4028–4032.

Fair, D. A., Cohen, A. L., Power, J. D., Dosenbach, N. U. F., Church, J. A., Miezin, F. M., Schlaggar, B. L., & Petersen, S. E. (2009). Functional brain networks develop from a "local to distributed" organization. *PLoS Computational Biology* **5**(5), e1000381.

Fair, D. A., Dosenbach, N. U. F., Church, J. A., Cohen, A. L., Brahmbhatt, S., Miezin, F. M., Barch, D. M., Raichle, M. E., Petersen, S. E., & Schlaggar, B. L. (2007). Development of distinct control networks through segregation and integration. *Proceedings of the National Academy of Sciences*, **104**(33), 13507–13512.

Faubel, C., & Schöner, G. (2008). Learning to recognize objects on the fly: A neurally based dynamic field approach. *Neural Networks*, **21**(4), 562–576.

Fisher, A. V. (2011). Automatic shifts of attention in the Dimensional Change Card Sort task: Subtle changes in task materials lead to flexible switching. *Journal of Experimental Child Psychology*, **108**, 211–219.

Fisher, A. V., & Sloutsky, V. M. (2005). When induction meets memory: Evidence for gradual transition from similarity-based to category based induction. *Child Development*, **76**(3), 583–597.

Forstmann, B. U., Wagenmakers, E., Eichele, T., Brown, S., & Serences, J. T. (2011). Reciprocal relations between cognitive neuroscience and cognitive models: Opposites attract? *Trends in Cognitive Science*, **15**(6), 272–279.

Friston, K. J. (2009). Modalities, modes, and models in functional neural imaging. *Science*, **326**, 399–403.

Frye, D., Zelazo, P. D., & Palfai, T. (1995). Theory of mind and rule-based reasoning. *Cognitive Development*, **10**, 483–527.

Garon, N., Bryson, S. E., & Smith, I. M. (2008). Executive function in preschoolers: A review using an integrative framework. *Psychological Bulletin*, **134**(1), 31–60.

Gathercole, S. E., Pickering, S. J., Knight, C., & Stegmann, Z. (2004). Working memory skills and educational attainment: Evidence from national curriculum assessments at 7 and 14 years of age. *Applied Cognitive Psychology*, **18**, 1–16.

Giedd, J. N., Blumenthal, J., Jeffries, N. O., Castellanos, F. X., Liu, H., Zijdenbos, A., Paus, T., Evans, A. C., & Rapoport, J. L. (1999). Brain development during childhood and adolescence: A longitudinal MRI study. *Nature Neuroscience*, **2**(10), 861–863.

Georgopolous, A. P., Schwartz, A. B., & Kettner, R. E. (1986). Neuronal population coding of movement direction. *Science*, **233**, 1416–1419.

Gerardi-Caulton, G. (2000). Sensitivity to spatial conflict and the development of self-regulation in children 24–36 months of age. *Developmental Science*, **3**(4), 397–404.

Geurts, H. M., Verté, S., Oosterlaan, J., Roeyers, H., & Sergeant, J. A. (2004). How specific are executive functioning deficits in attention deficit hyperactivity disorder and autism? *The Journal of Child Psychology and Psychiatry*, **45**(4), 836–854.

Gogtay, N., Giedd, J. N., Lusk, L., Hayashi, K. M., Greenstein, D., Vaituzis, A. C., Nugent, T. F., Herman, D. H., Clasen, L. S., Toga, A. W., Rapoport, J. L., & Thompson, P. M. (2004). Dynamic mapping of human cortical development during childhood through early adulthood. *Proceedings of the National Academy of Sciences*, **101**(21), 8174–8179.

Halford, G. S., Bunch, K., & McCredden, J. E. (2007). Problem decomposability as a factor in complexity of the dimensional change card sort. *Cognitive Development*, **22**(3), 384–391.

Happé, F., Booth, R., Charlton, R., & Hughes, C. (2006). Executive function deficits in autism spectrum disorders and attention-deficit/hyperactivity disorder: Examining profiles across domains and ages. *Brain and Cognition*, **61**, 25–39.

Harm, M. W., & Seidenberg, M. S. (1999). Phonology, reading acquisition, and dyslexia: Insights from connectionist models. *Psychological Review*, **106**(3), 491–528.

Harrison, S. A., & Tong, F. (2009). Decoding reveals the contents of visual working memory in early visual areas. *Nature*, **458**, 632–635.

Haxby, J. V., Grady, C. L., Horwitz, B., Ungerleider, L. G., Mishkin, M., Carson, R. E., Herscovitch, P., Schapiro, M. B., & Rapoport, S. I. (1991). Dissociation of object and spatial visual processing pathways in human extrastriate cortex. *Proceedings of the National Academy of Sciences*, **88**, 1621–1625.

Herd, S., Banich, M. T., & O'Reilly, R. C. (2006). Neural mechanisms of cognitive control: An integrative model of Stroop task performance and fMRI data. *Journal of Cognitive Neuroscience*, **18**(1), 22–32.

Honomichl, R. D., & Chen, Z. (2011). Relations as rules: The role of attention in the Dimensional Change Card Sort task. *Developmental Psychology*, **47**(1), 50–60.

Hughes, C., & Ensor, R. (2007). Executive function and theory of mind: Predictive relations from ages 2 to 4. *Developmental Psychology*, **43**(6), 1447–1459.

Huizinga, M., Dolan, C. V., & van der Molen, M. W. (2006). Age-related changes in executive function: Developmental trends and a latent variable analysis. *Neuropsychologia*, **44**, 2017–2036.

Hwang, K., Velanova, K., & Luna, B. (2010). Strengthening of top-down frontal cognitive control networks underlying the development of inhibitory control: A functional magnetic resonance imaging effective connectivity study. *The Journal of Neuroscience*, **30**(46), 15535–15545.

Im-Bolter, N., Johnson, J., & Pascual-Leone, J. (2006). Processing limitations in children with specific language impairment: The role of executive function. *Child Development*, **77**(6), 1822–1841.

Isaacs, E. B., & Vargha-Khadem, F. (1989). Differential course of development of spatial and verbal memory span: A normative study. *British Journal of Developmental Psychology*, **7**(4), 377–380.

Jancke, D., Erlhagen, W., Dinse, H. R., Akhavan, A. C., Giese, M., Steinhage, A., & Schöner, G. (1999). Parametric population representation of retinal location: Neuronal interaction dynamics in cat primary visual cortex. *The Journal of Neuroscience*, **19**(20), 9016–9028.

Joanisse, M. F., & Seidenberg, M. S. (2003). Phonology and syntax in specific language impairment: Evidence from a connectionist model. *Brain and Language*, **86**(1), 40–56.

Johnson, J. S., Spencer, J. P., Luck, S. J., & Schöner, G. (2009). A dynamic neural field model of visual working memory and change detection. *Psychological Science*, **20**(5), 568–577.

Johnson, J. S., Spencer, J. P., & Schöner, G. (2009). A layered neural architecture for the consolidation, maintenance, and updating of representations in visual working memory. *Brain Research*, **1299**, 17–32.

Johnson, J. S., Spencer, J. P., & Schöner, G. (2008). Moving to higher ground: The Dynamic Field Theory and the dynamics of visual cognition. In F. Garzòn, A. Laakso, & T. Gomila (Eds.), *Dynamics and Psychology New Ideas in Psychology*, **26**, 227–251 [special issue].

Jordan, P. J., & Morton, J. B. (2008). Flankers facilitate 3-year-olds' performance in a card-sorting task. *Developmental Psychology*, **44**(1), 263–274.

Kelly, A. M. C., Di Martino, A., Uddin, L. Q., Shehzad, Z., Gee, D. G., Reiss, P. T., Margulies, D. S., Castellanos, F. X., & Milham, M. P. (2009). Development of anterior cingulate functional connectivity from late childhood to early adulthood. *Cerebral Cortex*, **19**, 640–657.

Kelso, J. A. S., Scholz, J. P., & Schöner, G. (1988). Dynamics govern switching among patterns of coordination in biological movement. *Physics Letters A*, **134**, 8–12.

Kirkham, N. Z., Cruess, L., & Diamond, A. (2003). Helping children apply their knowledge to their behavior on a dimension-switching task. *Developmental Science*, **6**, 449–467.

Klingberg, T., Forssberg, H., & Westerberg, H. (2002). Increased brain activity in frontal and parietal cortex underlies the development of visuospatial working memory capacity during childhood. *Journal of Cognitive Neuroscience*, **14**(1), 1–10.

Kloo, D., & Perner, J. (2005). Disentangling dimensions in the dimensional change card sort task. *Developmental Science*, **8**(1), 44–56.

Kloo, D., Perner, J., Kerschhuber, A., Dabernig, S., & Aichhorn, M. (2008). Sorting between dimensions: Conditions of cognitive flexibility in preschoolers. *Journal of Experimental Child Psychology*, **100**, 115–134.

Kochanska, G., Coy, K. C., & Murray, K. T. (2001). The development of self-regulation in the first four years of life. *Child Development*, **72**(4), 1091–1111.

Kopecz, K., & Schöner, G. (1995). Saccadic motor planning by integrating visual information and pre-information on neural dynamic fields. *Biological Cybernetics*, **73**(1), 49–60.

Kourtzi, Z., Erb, M., Grodd, W., & Bülthoff, H. H. (2003). Representation of the perceived 3-D object shape in human lateral occipital complex. *Cerebral Cortex*, **13**, 911–920.

Kravitz, D. J., Vinson, L. D., & Baker, C. I. (2008). How position dependent is visual object recognition? *Trends in Cognitive Sciences*, **12**(3), 114–122.

Lehto, J. E., Juujärvi, P., Kooistra, L., & Pulkkinen, L. (2003). Dimensions of executive functioning: Evidence from children. *British Journal of Developmental Psychology*, **21**(1), 59–80.

Lenroot, R. K., & Giedd, J. N. (2006). Brain development in children and adolescents: Insights from anatomical magnetic resonance imaging. *Neuroscience & Biobehavioral Review*, **30**(6), 718–729.

Lepsien, J., & Nobre, A. C. (2007). Attentional modulation of object representations in working memory. *Cerebral Cortex*, **17**, 2072–2083.

Lipinski, J., Simmering, V. R., Johnson, J. S., & Spencer, J. P. (2010). The role of experience in location estimation: Target distributions shift location memory biases. *Cognition*, **115**(1), 147–153.

Lipinski, J., Spencer, J. P., & Samuelson, L. K. (2010). Biased feedback in spatial recall yields a violation of delta rule learning. *Psychonomic Bulletin and Review*, **17**, 581–588.

Liss, M., Fein, D., Allen, D., Dunn, M., Feinstein, C., Morris, R., Waterhouse, L., & Rapin, I. (2001). Executive functioning in high-functioning children with autism. *Journal of Child Psychology and Psychiatry*, **42**(2), 261–270.

Logie, R. H., & Pearson, D. G. (1997). The inner eye and the inner scribe of visuo-spatial working memory: Evidence from developmental fractionation. *The European Journal of Cognitive Psychology*, **9**(3), 241–257.

Logothetis, N. K., Pauls, J., Augath, M., Trinath, T., & Oeltermann, A. (2001). Neurophysiological investigation of the basis of the fMRI signal. *Nature*, **412**, 150–157.

Luck, S. J., & Vecera, S. P. (2002). Attention. In H. Pashler (Series Ed.) & S. Yantis (Volume Ed.), *Stevens' handbook of experimental psychology: Vol. 1. Sensation and perception* (3rd ed., pp. 235–286.). New York: Wiley.

Luck, S. J., & Vogel, E. K. (1997). The capacity of visual working memory for features and conjunctions. *Nature*, **390**, 279–281.

Mack, W. (2007). Improving postswitch performance in the dimensional change card-sorting task: The importance of the switch and of pretraining by redescribing the test cards. *Journal of Experimental Child Psychology*, **98**, 243–251.

Marcovitch, S., Boseovski, J. J., & Knapp, R. J. (2007). Use it or lose it: Examining preschoolers' difficulty in maintaining and executing a goal. *Developmental Science*, **10**(5), 559–564.

Marcovitch, S., & Zelazo, P. D. (1999). The A-not-B error: Evidence from a logistic meta-analysis. *Child Development*, **70**(6), 1297–1313.

Markounikau, V., Igel, C., Grinvald, A., & Jancke, D. (2010). A dynamic neural field model of mesoscopic cortical activity captured with voltage-sensitive dye imaging. *PLoS Computational Biology*, **6**(9), e1000919.

Mazocco, M. M. M., & Kover, S. T. (2007). A longitudinal assessment of executive function skills and their associations with math performance. *Child Neuropsychology*, **13**, 18–45.

McDowell, K., Jeka, J. J., Schöner, G., & Hatfield, B. D. (2002). Behavioral and electrophysiological evidence of an interaction between probability and task metrics in movement preparation. *Experimental Brain Research*, **144**(3), 303–313.

McEvoy, R. E., Rogers, S. J., & Pennington, B. F. (1993). Executive function and social communication deficits in young autistic children. *Journal of Child Psychology and Psychiatry*, **34**(4), 563–578.

McMurray, B., Samelson, V. M., Lee, S. H., & Tomblin, J. B. (2010). Individual differences in online spoken word recognition: Implications for SLI. *Cognitive Psychology*, **60**(1), 1–39.

McNab, F., Leroux, G., Strand, F., Thorell, L., Bergman, S., & Klingberg, T. (2008). Common and unique components of inhibition and working memory: An fMRI within-subject investigation. *Neuropsychologia*, **46**, 2668–2682.

Meyer, D. E., & Kieras, D. E. (1997). A computational theory of executive cognitive processes and multiple-task performance: Part I. Basic mechanisms. *Psychological Review*, **104**(1), 3–65.

Milner, B. (1963). Effects of different brain lesions on card sorting: The role of the frontal lobes. *Archives of Neurology*, **9**(1), 90–100.

Minati, L., Visani, E., Dowell, N. G., Medford, N., & Critchley, H. D. (2011). Variability comparison of simultaneous brain near-infrared spectroscopy (NIRS) and functional MRI (fMRI) during visual stimulation. *Journal of Medical Engineering Technology*, **35**, 370–376.

Miyake, A., Friedman, N. P., Emerson, M. J., Witzki, A. H., & Howerter, A. (2000). The unity and diversity of executive functions and their contributions to complex "frontal lobe" tasks: A latent variable analysis. *Cognitive Psychology*, **41**, 49–100.

Moffitt, T. E., Arseneault, L., Belsky, D., Dickson, N., Hancox, R. J., Harrignton, H., Houts, R., Poulton, R., Roberts, B. W., Ross, S., Sears, M. R., Thomson, W. M., & Caspi, A. (2011). A gradient of childhood self-control predicts health, wealth, and public safety. *Proceedings of the National Academy of Sciences*, **108**(7), 2693–2698.

Moriguchi, Y., & Hiraki, K. (2009). Neural origins of cognitive shifting in young children. *Proceedings of the National Academy of Sciences*, **106**(14), 6017–6021.

Morton, J. B. (2010). Understanding genetic, neurophysiological, and experiential influences on the development of executive function: The need for developmental models. *Wiley Interdisciplinary Reviews: Cognitive Science*, **1**(5), 709–723.

Morton, J. B., Bosma, R., & Ansari, D. (2009). Age-related changes in brain activation associated with dimensional shifts of attention: An fMRI study. *Neuroimage*, **46**, 249–256.

Morton, J. B., & Munakata, Y. (2002). Active versus latent representations: A neural network model of perseveration and dissociation in early childhood. *Developmental Psychobiology*, **40**, 255–265.

Müller, U., Dick, A. S., Gela, K., Overton, W. F., & Zelazo, P. D. (2006). The role of negative priming in preschoolers' flexible rule use on the dimensional change card sort task. *Child Development*, **77**(2), 395–412.

Müller, U., Zelazo, P. D., Lurye, L. E., & Liebermann, D. P. (2008). The effect of labeling on preschool children's performance in the Dimensional Change Card Sort Task. *Cognitive Development*, **23**, 395–408.

Nagahama, Y., Okada, T., Katsumi, Y., Hayashi, T., Yamauchi, H., Oyanagi, C., Konishi, J., Fukuyama, H., & Shibasaki, H. (2001). Dissociable mechanisms of attentional control within the human prefrontal cortex. *Cerebral Cortex*, **11**(1), 85–92.

Norman, D. A., & Shallice, T. (1986). Attention to action: Willed and automatic control of behavior. In R. J. Davidson, G. E. Schwartz, & D. Shapiro (Eds.), *Consciousness and self-regulation: Advances in research and theory* (pp. 1–19). New York: Plenum Press.

Nosofsky, R. M. (1984). Choice, similarity, and the context theory of classification. *Journal of Experimental Psychology: Learning, Memory, & Cognition*, **10**, 104–114.

O'Reilly, R. C., Braver, T. S., & Cohen, J. D. (1999). A biologically based computational model of working memory. In A. Miyake & P. Shah (Eds.), *Models of working memory: Mechanisms of active maintenance and executive control* (pp. 375–411). New York: Cambridge University Press.

O'Reilly, R. C., & Frank, M. J. (2006). Making working memory work: A computational model of learning in the prefrontal cortex and basal ganglia. *Neural Computation*, **18**(2), 283–328.

Op De Beeck, H., & Vogels, R. (2000). Spatial sensitivity of macaque inferior temporal neurons. *Journal of Comparative Neurology*, **426**, 505–518.

Ozonoff, S., & McEvoy, R. E. (1994). A longitudinal study of executive function and theory of mind development in autism. *Developmental Psychopathology*, **6**, 415–431.

Pennington, B. F., & Ozonoff, S. (1996). Executive functions and developmental psychopathology. *The Journal of Child Psychology and Psychiatry*, **37**(1), 51–87.

Perner, J., & Lang, B. (2002). What causes 3-year-olds' difficulty on the dimensional change card sort task? *Infant and Child Development*, **11**(2), 93–105.

Perone, S. (in press). A process view of learning and development in an autonomous exploratory system. In J. P. Spencer & G. S. Schöner (Eds.), *Dynamic thinking—A primer on dynamic field theory*. New York, NY: Oxford University Press.

Perone, S., Simmering, V. R., & Spencer, J. P. (2011). Stronger neural dynamics capture changes in infants' visual working memory capacity over development. *Developmental Science*, **14**(6), 1379–1392.

Pessiglione, M., Seymour, B., Flandin, G., Dolan, R. J., & Frith, C. D. (2009). Dopamine-dependent prediction errors underpin reward-seeking behavior in humans. *Nature*, **442**, 1042–1045.

Pickering, S. J. (2001). Cognitive approaches to the fractionation of visuo-spatial working memory. *Cortex*, **37**(4), 457–473.

Plaut, D. C., McClelland, J. L., Seidenberg, M. S., & Patterson, K. (1996). Understanding normal and impaired word reading: Computational principles in quasi-regular domains. *Psychological Review*, **103**(1), 56–115.

Postle, B. R. (2006). Working memory as an emergent property of the mind and brain. *Neuroscience, 139*(1), 23–38.

Prince, M., Patel, V., Saxena, S., Maj, M., Maselko, J., Phillips, M. R., & Rahman, A. (2007). No health without metnal health. *Lancet, 370*, 859–877.

Rao, S. C., Rainer, G., & Miller, E. K. (1997). Integration of what and where in the primate prefrontal cortex. *Science, 276*, 821–824.

Rennie, D. A. C., Bull, R., & Diamond, A. (2004). Executive functioning in preschoolers: Reducing the inhibitory demands of the dimensional change card sort task. *Developmental Neuropsychology, 26*(1), 423–443.

Roberts, R. J., Hager, L. D., & Heron, C. (1994). Prefrontal cognitive processes: Working memory and inhibition in the antisaccade task. *Journal of Experimental Psychology: General, 123*(4), 374–393.

Roberts, R. J., & Pennington, B. F. (1996). An interactive framework for examining prefrontal cognitive process. *Developmental Neuropsychology, 12*(1), 105–126.

Rueda, M. R., Fan, J., McCandliss, B. D., Halparin, J. D., Gruber, D. B., Lercari, L. P., & Posner, M. I. (2004). Development of attentional networks in childhood. *Neuropsychologia, 42*(8), 1029–1040.

Samuelson, L. K., Schutte, A. R., & Horst, J. S. (2009). The dynamic nature of knowledge: Insights from a dynamic field model of children's novel noun generalization. *Cognition, 110*(3), 322–345.

Samuelson, L. K., & Smith, L. B. (1999). Early noun vocabularies: Do ontology, category structure and syntax correspond? *Cognition, 73*, 1–33.

Samuelson, L. K., Smith, L. B., Perry, L. K., & Spencer, J. P. (2011). Grounding word learning in space. *PLoS ONE, 6*, e28095.

Sandamirskaya, Y., & Schöner, G. (2010). An embodied account of serial order: How instabilities drive sequence generation. *Neural Networks, 23*(10), 1164–1179.

Sandhofer, C. M., & Smith, L. B. (1999). Learning color words involves learning a system of mappings. *Developmental Psychology, 35*(3), 668–697.

Sandhofer, C. M., & Smith, L. B. (2001). Why children learn color and size words so differently: Evidence from adults' learning of artificial terms. *Journal of Experimental Psychology: General, 130*(4), 600–620.

Schneegans, S., Lins, J., Spencer, J. P. (in press). Integration and selection in dynamic fields: Moving beyond a single dimension. In J. P. Spencer & G. S. Schöner (Eds.), *Dynamic thinking—A primer on dynamic field theory*. New York, NY: Oxford University Press.

Schneider, W., Lockl, K., & Fernandez, O. (2005). Interrelationships among theory of mind, executive control, language development, and working memory in young children: A longitudinal analysis. In W. Schneider, R. Schumann-Hengsteler, & B. Sodian (Eds.), *Young children's cognitive development: Interrelations among executive functioning, working memory, verbal ability, and theory of mind* (pp. 259–284). Hillsdale, NJ: Lawrence Erlbaum.

Schöner, G. (2009). Development as change of system dynamics: Stability, instability, and emergence. In J. P. Spencer, M. S. C. Thomas, & J. L. McClelland (Eds.), *Toward a new grand theory of development? Connectionism and dynamic systems theory reconsidered* (pp. 25–47). New York, NY: Oxford University Press.

Schöner, G., & Kelso, J. A. S. (1988). Dynamic pattern generation in behavioral and neural systems. *Science, 239*, 1513–1520.

Schroeter, M. L., Zysset, S., Wahl, M., & von Cramon, D. Y. (2004). Prefrontal activation due to Stroop interference increases during development—An event-related fNIRS study. *Neuroimage*, **23**(4), 1317–1325.

Schutte, A. R., & Spencer, J. R. (2009). Tests of the dynamic field theory and the spatial precision hypothesis: Capturing a qualitative developmental transition in spatial working memory. *Journal of Experimental Psychology: Human Perception and Performance*, **35**(6), 1689–1725.

Schutte, A. R., Spencer, J. P., & Schöner, G. (2003). Testing the dynamic field theory: Working memory for locations becomes more spatially precise over development. *Child Development*, **74**(5), 1393–1417.

Silver, M. A., & Kastner, S. (2009). Topographic maps in human frontal and parietal cortex. *Trends in Cognitive Science*, **13**(11), 488–495.

Simmering, V. A. (2008). *Developing a magic number: The dynamic field theory reveals why visual working capacity estimates differ across tasks and development.* Iowa City, IA: University of Iowa.

Simmering, V. A. (2011). The development of visual working memory capacity during early childhood. *Journal of Experimental Child Psychology*, **111**, 695–707.

Simmering, V. A., Schutte, A. R., & Spencer, J. P. (2008). Generalizing the dynamic field theory of spatial cognition across real and developmental time scales. In S. Becker (Ed.). *Computational Cognitive Neuroscience Brain Research*, **1202**, 68–86 [special issue].

Simmons, W. K., Ramjee, V., Beauchamp, M. S., McRae, A., Martin, A., & Barsalou, L. W. (2007). A common neural substrate for perceiving and knowing about color. *Neuropsychologia*, **45**, 2802–2810.

Smith, L. B., Jones, S. S., & Landau, B. (1996). Naming in young children: A dumb attentional mechanism? *Cognition*, **60**(2), 143–171.

Smith, L. B., Thelen, E., Titzer, R., & McLin, D. (1999). Knowing in the context of acting: The task dynamics of the A-not-B error. *Psychological Review*, **106**(2), 235–260.

Sowell, E. R., Trauner, D. A., Garnst, A., & Jernigan, T. L. (2002). Development of cortical and subcortical brain structures in childhood and adolescence: A structural MRI study. *Developmental Medicine & Child Neurology*, **44**(1), 4–16.

Spencer, J. P., Austin, A., & Schutte, A. R (2012). Contributions of dynamic systems theory to cognitive development. *Cognitive Development*, **27**, 401–418.

Spencer, J. P., Barich, K., Goldberg, J., & Perone, S. (2012). Behavioral dynamics and neural grounding of a dynamic field theory of multi-object tracking. *Journal of Integrative Neuroscience*, **11**, 339–362.

Spencer, J. P., & Buss, A. T (under review). The emergent executive: A dynamic neural field model of the development of cognitive control. In P. D. Zelazo & M. Sera (Eds.), *The Minnesota Symposium on Child Psychology, Vol. 37. Developing Cognitive Control Processes: Mechanisms, Implications, and Interventions.*

Spencer, J. P., Perone, S., & Johnson, J. S. (2009). Dynamic field theory and embodied cognitive dynamics. In J. P. Spencer, M. Thomas, & J. L. McClelland (Eds.), *Toward a unified theory of development: Connectionism and dynamic systems theory re-considered.* New York: Oxford University Press.

Spencer, J. P., Schneegans, S., & Schöner, G. (in press). Integrating "what" and "where": Visual working memory for objects in a scene. In J. P. Spencer & G. S. Schöner (Eds.), *Dynamic Thinking—A Primer on Dynamic Field Theory.* New York, NY: Oxford University Press.

Stedron, J. M., Sahni, S. D., & Munakata, Y. (2005). Common mechanisms for working memory and attention: The case of perseveration with visible solutions. *Journal of Cognitive Neuroscience*, **17**(4), 623–631.

Stevens, M. C., Pearlson, G. D., & Caloun, V. D. (2009). Changes in the interaction of resting-state neural networks from adolescence to adulthood. *Human Brain Mapping*, **30**, 2356–2366.

Stevens, M. C., Skudlarski, P., Pearlson, G. D., & Calhoun, V. D. (2009). Age-related cognitive gains are mediated by the effects of white matter development on brain integration. *Neuroimage*, **48**, 738–746.

Thelen, E., Schöner, G., Scheier, C., & Smith, L. (2001). The dynamics of embodiment: A field theory of infant perseverative reaching. *Behavioral and Brain Sciences*, **24**, 1–86.

Thelen, E., & Smith, L. B. (1994). *A dynamic systems approach to cognition and action*. Cambridge, MA: MIT Press.

Thomason, M. E., Race, E., Burrows, B., Whitfield-Gabrieli, S., Glover, G. H., & Gabrieli, J. D. E. (2009). Development of spatial and verbal working memory capacity in the human brain. *Journal of Cognitive Neuroscience*, **21**(2), 316–332.

Towse, J. N., Redbond, J., Houston-Price, C. M. T., & Cook, S. (2000). Understanding the dimensional change card sort: Perspectives from task success and failure. *Cognitive Development*, **15**, 347–365.

Treisman, A. M. (1996). The binding problem. *Current Opinions in Neurobiology*, **6**(2), 171–178.

Treisman, A. M., & Gelade, G. (1980). A feature-integration theory of attention. *Cognitive Psychology*, **12**, 97–136.

Tsujii, T., Yamamoto, E., Masuda, S., & Watanabe, S. (2009). Longitudinal study of spatial working memory development in young children. *Neuroreport*, **20**(8), 759–763.

Tsujimoto, S. (2008). The prefrontal cortex: Functional neural development during early childhood. *The Neuroscientist*, **14**, 345–358.

Turvey, M. T., & Shaw, R. E. (1995). Toward an ecological physics and a physical psychology. In R. Solso & D. Massaro (Eds.), *The science of the mind: 2001 and beyond* (pp. 144–169). Oxford: Oxford University Press.

Ungerleider, L. G., & Mishkin, M. (1982). Two cortical visual systems. In D. J. Ingle, M. A. Goodale, & R. J. W. Mansfield (Eds.), *Analysis of visual behavior* (pp. 549–586). Cambridge, MA: MIT Press.

Vicari, S., Bellucci, S., & Carlesimo, G. A. (2003). Visual and spatial working memory dissociation: Evidence from Williams syndrome. *Developmental Medicine & Child Neurology*, **45**(4), 269–273.

Waxer, M., & Morton, J. B. (2011). Multiple processes underlying dimensional change card sort performance: A developmental electrophysiological investigation. *Journal of Cognitive Neuroscience*, **23**(11), 3267–3279.

Wiebe, S. A., Sheffield, T., Nelson, J. M., Clark, C. A. C., Chevalier, N., & Espy, K. A. (2011). The structure of executive function in 3-year-olds. *Journal of Experimental Child Psychology*, **108**, 436–452.

Wilson, H. R., & Cowan, J. D. (1972). Excitatory and inhibitory interactions in localized populations of model neurons. *Biophysical Journal*, **12**, 1–24.

Xiao, Y.-P., Wang, Y., & Felleman, D. J. (2003). A spatially organized representation of color in macaque cortical area V2. *Nature*, **421**, 532–539.

Yerys, B., & Munakata, Y. (2006). When labels hurt but novelty helps: Children's perseveration and flexibility in a card-sorting task. *Child Development*, **77**(6), 1589–1607.

Zanto, T. P., Rubens, M. T., Bollinger, J., & Gazzaley, A. (2010). Top-down modulation of visual feature processing: The role of the inferior frontal junction. *NeuroImage*, **53**, 736–745.

Zanto, T. P., Rubens, M. T., Thangavel, A., & Gazzaley, A. (2011). Causal role of the prefrontal cortex in top-down modulation of visual processing and working memory. *Nature Neuroscience*, **14**, 656–663.

Zelazo, P. D. (2004). The development of conscious control in childhood. *Trends in Cognitive Sciences*, **8**(1), 12–17.

Zelazo, P. D., Frye, D., & Rapus, T. (1996). An age-related dissociated between knowing rules and using them. *Cognitive Development*, **11**, 37–63.

Zelazo, P. D., Müller, U., Frye, D., & Markovitch, S. (2003). The development of executive function in early childhood. *Monographs for the Society for Research in Child Development*, **68**(3), vii-137.

Zelazo, P. D., Reznick, J. S., & Piñon, D. E. (1995). Response control and the execution of verbal rules. *Developmental Psychology*, **31**(3), 508–517.

Model Equations

The basic formulation for a one-dimensional neural field tuned to, for instance, spatial information is given in Equation (1). The rate of change of activation in a cortical field, w, evolves over time, t, at each location in the field, x.

$$\tau_w \dot{w}(x, t) = -w(x, t) + h_w + S(x, t) + \int c_{ww}(x - x')\Lambda(w(x', t))\mathrm{d}x'$$
$$+ \int c_{wv}(x - x')\Lambda(v(x', t))\mathrm{d}x' \tag{1}$$

The first part of Equation (1), underlined with a dotted line, captures the neural resting level ($h_w < 0$), stimulus input at particular locations presented at specific times in an experiment ($S(x, t)$), and a stabilization term ($-w(x, t)$). The resting level determines how far a field is from the activation threshold. The stabilizing term serves to maintain activation around an attractor state. That is, as the system is pushed away from its stable state, the rate of change goes in the opposite direction of the perturbation. Note that the tau parameter, τ_w, captures the timescale at which activation approaches the attractor state.

The remainder of the equation specifies the excitatory (section underlined with a dashed line) and inhibitory neural interactions (portion underlined with a solid line). Neural interactions within a field are determined by the convolution of a sigmoidal threshold function and a Gaussian projection. The term $\Lambda(w(x, t))$ is the sigmoided value of activation at each location in the working memory (WM) field (w) used for the self-excitatory projection, while $\Lambda(v(x, t))$ is the sigmoided value of activation at each point in the Inhib field (v) used for the inhibitory projection into the WM field. The sigmoid function is given by Equation (2).

$$\Lambda(w) = \frac{1}{1 + \exp[-\beta w]} \tag{2}$$

The β parameter defines the slope of the sigmoid function that transforms field activation into neural output. Here, the activation threshold is represented by the point where the sigmoided output reaches 0.5, which is 0. With a large β value, the slope is steeper and there is a more abrupt transition in the sigmoided output, approaching a step function. Thus, weak levels of activation in the field contribute relatively little to activation and peak formation, while strong levels of activation in the fields engage in robust interactions with associated neurons.

The spread and strength of neural interactions is determined by a Gaussian interaction kernel, which is generically defined in Equation (3).

$$c(x - x') = c \exp\left[\frac{(x - x')^2}{2\sigma^2}\right] \tag{3}$$

The parameter denoted by c scales the strength of the projection while the width of the interaction kernel is given by σ. Finally, these terms are integrated to combine the contributions at each location, x, from all other locations, x' (see Equation 1).

The equation for the inhibitory layer takes the same general form as the equation for the WM field and is given by Equation (4):

$$\tau_v \dot{v}(x, t) = -v(x, t) + h_v + \int c_{vw}(x - x') \, \Lambda(w(x', t)) \mathrm{d}x' \tag{4}$$

The timescale of activation in this field is given by τ_v while its resting level is denoted h_v. In this equation, input to the inhibitory layer is the integration of above-threshold activation within the WM field, $\Lambda(w(x, t))$, with the spread and strength of this projection given by the Gaussian interaction kernel, $c_{vw}(x - x')$.

A further contribution to the dynamics in the WM field comes from a Hebbian layer (HL) which is now added in Equation (5).

$$t_w \dot{w}(x, t) = -w(x, t) + h_w + S(x, t) + \int c_{ww}(x - x') \, \Lambda(w(x, t)) \mathrm{d}x'$$
$$+ \int c_{wv}(x - x') \, \Lambda(v(x, t)) \mathrm{d}x' + \int c_{HL}(x - x') w_{HL}(x, t) \mathrm{d}x' \tag{5}$$

The Gaussian interaction kernel, $c_{HL}(x - x')$, determines the strength and width of the projection from the HL into the WM field. The dynamics of the HL (w_{HL}; Equation 6.0) are divided into two components (Equations 6.1 and 6.2) that capture the build and decay dynamics of HL separately:

$$\dot{w}_{HL}(x, t) = \dot{w}_{HLbuild}(x, t) + \dot{w}_{HLdecay}(x, t) \tag{6}$$

$$\tau_{build} \dot{w}_{HLbuild}(x, t) = [-w_{HL}(x, t) + \Lambda(w(x, t))] \cdot \theta(w(x, t)) \tag{6.1}$$

$$\tau_{decay} \dot{w}_{HLdecay}(x, t) = -w_{HL}(x, t) \cdot [1 - \theta(w(x, t))] \tag{6.2}$$

The shunting term, θ, gates activation into the HL from the WM field ($\theta = 1$ when $w(x, t) > 0$, and $\theta = 0$ otherwise). With $\theta = 1$, Equation (6.1) is engaged and drives the accumulation of activation in the HL at sites associated with above-threshold activation in the WM field. By contrast, when $\theta = 0$, Equation (6.2) is engaged and activation levels in the HL decay. Separating the build and decay mechanisms approximates accumulation and depression of synaptic change (Deco & Rolls, 2004). The build timescale (e.g., $\tau_{\text{biild}} = 200$) is shorter than the decay timescale (e.g., $\tau_{\text{decay}} = 1,000$), which makes activation in the HL build more quickly relative to the rate of decay; however, both of these are significantly slower than the timescale for the WM field (i.e., $\tau = 40$). Thus, as inputs are presented to the WM field and peaks of activation are built, activation accumulates slowly in the HL. This accumulated activation acts as an input to the WM field, which can have various influences on the stability properties of this field. This source of activation can make particular modes of behavior more stable than others, build up biases, or make peaks of activation build more quickly.

The Object WM Model

In this section we describe the equations governing activation in the full object representation model used to quantitatively fit 3- and 5-year-olds behavior in the DCCS. The parameters for the excitatory and inhibitory field dynamics are given in Table A1. The parameters for the spatial interactions among the WM fields are given in Table A2. The spatial WM field is given by Equation (7).

TABLE A1

FIELD PARAMETERS AND LATERAL INTERACTION STRENGTHS

Resting Level	Lateral Excitation	Lateral Inhibition	Global Inhibition
$h_{\text{ws}} = -4$	$c_{\text{ww}} = 0.9$	$c_{\text{wvs}} = 1.75$	$c_{\text{wvsg}} = 0.4$
$h_{\text{vs}} = -4$	$c_{\text{vws}} = 1.35$		
$h_{\text{wf1}} = -7$	$c_{\text{wwf1}} = 0.7$	$c_{\text{wvf1}} = 0.3$	$c_{\text{wvf1g}} = 0.5$
$h_{\text{vf1}} = -4$	$c_{\text{vwf1}} = 0.65$		
$h_{\text{wf2}} = -7$	$c_{\text{wwf2}} = 0.7$	$c_{\text{wvf2}} = 0.3$	$c_{\text{wvf2g}} = 0.5$
$h_{\text{vf2}} = -4$	$c_{\text{vwf2}} = 0.65$		

Note. The time constant for all working memory (WM) fields (w) is $\tau = 40$ while the time constant for all inhibitory fields (v) is $\tau = 5$. The lateral excitation width are $\sigma_{\text{wws}} = \sigma_{\text{wwf1}} = \sigma_{\text{wwf2}} = 3$ and the lateral inhibition width are $\sigma_{\text{wvs}} = \sigma_{\text{wvf1}} = \sigma_{\text{wvf2}} = 20$. The sigmoid steepness for all if the local-excitatory and laterally inhibitory interactions within the fields is $\beta_{\text{wws}} = \beta_{\text{wvs}} = \beta_{\text{vws}} = \beta_{\text{wwf1}} = \beta_{\text{wvf1}} = \beta_{\text{vwf1}} = \beta_{\text{wwf2}} = \beta_{\text{wvf2}} = \beta_{\text{vwf2}} = 5$. The parameters for the Hebbian layer are: $\text{HL}_{\text{build}} = 500$, $\text{HL}_{\text{decay}} = 2,000$, $c_{\text{HL}} = 0.065$, $\sigma_{\text{HLfeature}} = 5$, $\sigma_{\text{HLspace}} = 10$.

TABLE A2

PARAMETERS OF SPATIAL INTERACTIONS BETWEEN FIELDS

Excitatory Strength	Kernel Width
$c_{wswf1} = 0.2$	$\sigma_{wswf1} = 2$
$c_{wswf2} = 0.2$	$\sigma_{wswf2} = 2$
$c_{wf1ws} = 0.1$	$\sigma_{wf1ws} = 2$
$c_{wf2ws} = 0.1$	$\sigma_{wf2ws} = 2$
$c_{wf1wf2} = 0.35$	$\sigma_{wf1wf2} = 2$
$c_{wf2wf1} = 0.35$	$\sigma_{wf2wf1} = 2$

Note. The sigmoid steepness for all interactions between fields is $\beta_{wsf1} = \beta_{wsf2} = \beta_{wf1ws} = \beta_{wf2ws} = \beta_{wf1wf2} = \beta_{wf2wf1} = 1$.

$$
\begin{aligned}
\tau_{w_s} \dot{w}_s(x, t) = {} & -w(x, t) + h_s + \int c_{ww_s}(x - x')\Lambda(w_s(x', t))\mathrm{d}x' \\
& + \int c_{w_x v_s}(x - x')\Lambda(v_s(x', t))\mathrm{d}x' \\
& + \int c_{w_s w_{f1}}(x - x')\Lambda(w_{f1}(x', t))\mathrm{d}x' \\
& + \int c_{w_s w_{f2}}(x - x')\Lambda(w_{f2}(x', t))\mathrm{d}x' \\
& + \int c_{w_s w_{HL}}(x - x')w_{HL}(x', t)\mathrm{d}x' \\
& + \int c_{w_s \text{noise}}(x - x')\xi(x, t)\mathrm{d}x'
\end{aligned}
\tag{7}
$$

$\dot{w}_s(x, t)$ specifies the rate of change of the field at every location, x, along the spatial dimension as a function of time. The constant τ_{w_s} determines the time scale of the dynamics (Erlhagen & Schöner, 2002), while $-w(x, t)$ is the stabilizing term that serves to drive activation toward h_{w_s}, the resting-level of the field. Next, the field is influenced by the self-excitatory and laterally inhibitory projections, $\int c_{ww_s}(x - x')\,\Lambda(w_s(x', t))\mathrm{d}x'$ and $\int c_{w_s v_s}(x - x')\Lambda(v_s(x', t))\mathrm{d}x'$, respectively. Projections between fields are defined as the convolution of a sigmoid function (e.g., $\Lambda(w_s(x', t))$) with the Gaussian interaction kernel (e.g., $c_{ww_s}(x - x')$).

The next terms in Equation (7) are the projections of activation from w_{f1} and w_{f2} (the color and shape WM fields, respectively) into w_s. These are followed by the influence from accumulated HTs, $\int c_{w_s w_{HL}}(x - x')w_{HL}(x', t)\mathrm{d}x'$, and spatially correlated noise added to the field.

The inhibitory layer for the spatial system is given by Equation (8):

$$\tau_v \dot{v}_s(x, t) = -v_s(x, t) + h_{v_s} + \int c_{v,w_s}(x - x')\,\Lambda(w(x', t))\mathrm{d}x' + \int c_{v,\text{noise}}(x - x')\xi(x, t)\mathrm{d}x$$

$$(8)$$

As with the equation for the WM field, $\dot{v}_s(x, t)$ is the rate of change of neural activity in the inhibitory field at every location, x, along the spatial dimension as a function of time. The term $-v_s(x, t)$ is a stabilizing influence that drives activation toward the resting level of the field, h_{v_s}. Input to this field comes from the convolution of the sigmoid of activation in the WM field, $\Lambda(w(x', t))$, with the Gaussian interaction kernel, $c_{v,w_s}(x - x')$. This field also has a spatially correlated stochastic influence. The dynamics of the HL for the spatial WM field are given by Equations (6.0)–(6.2) above.

The feature WM field (in this example, it is the color WM field) is given by Equation (9):

$$
\begin{aligned}
\tau \dot{w}_{f1}(x, y, t) = {}& -w_{f1}(x, y, t) + h_{w_{f1}} + S_{w_{f1}}(x, y, t) \\
& + \iint c_{ww_{f1}}(x - x', y - y')\Lambda(w_{f1}(x', y', t))\mathrm{d}x'\mathrm{d}y' \\
& + \iint c_{wv_{f1}}(x - x', y - y')\Lambda(v_{f1}(x', y', t))\mathrm{d}x'\mathrm{d}y' \\
& + \int c_{w_{f1}w_s}(x - x', y - y')\Lambda(w_s(x', t))\mathrm{d}x' \\
& + \iint c_{w_{f1}w_{f2}}(x - x', y - y')\Lambda(w_{f2}(x', y', t))\mathrm{d}x'\mathrm{d}y' \\
& + \iint c_{w_{f1}w_{\text{HL}_{f1}}}(x - x', y - y')w_{\text{HL}_{f1}}(x', y', t)\mathrm{d}x'\mathrm{d}y' \\
& + c_{wi_{\text{ColorColor}}}\Lambda(i_{\text{Color}}(t)) + c_{wi_{\text{ColorShape}}}\Lambda(i_{\text{Shape}}(t)) \\
& + \iint c_{w_{f1}\text{noise}}(x - x', y - y')\xi(x', y', t))\mathrm{d}x'\mathrm{d}y'
\end{aligned}
$$

$$(9)$$

The color WM fields have five excitatory inputs: a self-excitatory projection ($\iint c_{ww_{f1}}(x - x', y - y')\Lambda(w_{f1}(x', y', t))\mathrm{d}x'\mathrm{d}y'$), a projection from the spatial field ($\int c_{w_{f1}w_s}(x - x', y - y')\Lambda(w_s(x', t))\mathrm{d}x'$), a projection from the second feature field ($\iint c_{w_{f1}w_{f2}}(x - x', y - y')\Lambda(w_{f2}(x', y', t))\mathrm{d}x'\mathrm{d}y'$), a projection from its associated HL ($\iint c_{w_{f1}w_{\text{HL}_{f1}}}(x - x', y - y')w_{\text{HL}_{f1}}(x', y', t)\mathrm{d}x'\mathrm{d}y'$), and inputs from the "shape" and "color" nodes ($c_{wi_{\text{ColorColor}}}\Lambda(i_{\text{Color}}(t))$, $c_{wi_{\text{ColorShape}}}\Lambda(i_{\text{Shape}}(t))$). The projection from its associated inhibitory field is given by ($\iint c_{wv_{f1}}(x - x', y - y')\,\Lambda(v_{f1}(x', y', t))\mathrm{d}x'\mathrm{d}y'$). Finally, this field is influenced by two-dimensional spatially correlated noise.

The associated two-dimensional inhibitory field is given by Equation (10).

$$
\begin{aligned}
\tau_{v_{f1}} \dot{v}_{f1}(x, y, t) = {}& -v_{f1}(x, y, t) + h_{v_{f1}} + \iint c_{ww_{f1}}(x - x', y - y')\Lambda(w_{f1}(x', y', t))\mathrm{d}x'\mathrm{d}y' \\
& + \iint c_{v_{f1}\text{noise}}(x - x', y - y')\xi(x', y', t))\mathrm{d}x'\mathrm{d}y'
\end{aligned}
$$

$$(10)$$

The input to this field is the convolution of the sigmoid of activation in w_{f1} with a Gaussian interaction kernel ($\iint c_{ww_{f1}}(x - x', y - y') \Lambda(w_{f1}(x', y', t))\, dx'dy'$). The last term in this equation is the influence from two-dimensional spatially correlated noise.

The dynamics of HL in the 2D fields are governed by Equations (11.0)–(11.2). The parameters for these equations are given in Table A1.

$$\dot{w}_{\mathrm{HL}_{f1}}(x, y, t) = \dot{w}_{\mathrm{HLbuild}_{f1}}(x, y, t) + \dot{w}_{\mathrm{HLdecay}_{f1}}(x, y, t) \tag{11}$$

$$\tau_{\mathrm{build}}\,\dot{w}_{\mathrm{HLbuild}_{f1}}(x, y, t) = [w_{\mathrm{HL}_{f1}}(x, y, t) + \Lambda(w_{f1}(x, y, t))]$$
$$\cdot\, \theta(w_{f1}(x, y, t)) \tag{11.1}$$

$$\tau_{\mathrm{decay}}\,\dot{w}_{\mathrm{HLdecay}_{f1}}(x, y, t) = w_{\mathrm{HL}_{f1}}(x, y, t) \cdot [1 - \theta(w_{f1}(x, y, t))] \tag{11.2}$$

Note that the same equations govern activation in the shape WM, inhibitory, and HL fields (w_{f2}).

Finally, the dynamics of the "shape" and "color" nodes are given by Equations (12) and (13). The parameters relevant for these nodes are given in Table A3.

$$\tau \dot{i}_{\mathrm{shape}}(t) = -i_{\mathrm{shape}}(t) + h_{i_{\mathrm{shape}}} + S_{i_{\mathrm{shape}}}(t) + c_{ii_{\mathrm{excite}}} \Lambda(i_{\mathrm{shape}}(t))$$
$$- c_{ii_{\mathrm{inhib}}} \Lambda(i_{\mathrm{color}}(t)) + c_{iw\mathrm{ShapeColor}} \sum\sum \Lambda(w_{f1}(t)) \tag{12}$$
$$+ c_{iw\mathrm{ShapeShape}} \sum\sum \Lambda(w_{f2}(t))$$

TABLE A3

PARAMETERS FOR THE DIMENSIONAL ATTENTION NODES

3-Year-Old Model	4-Year-Old Model
$h_i = -4$	$h_i = -4$
$c_{\mathrm{ii\_excite}} = 1$	$c_{\mathrm{ii\_excite}} = 5$
$c_{\mathrm{ii\_inhib}} = 5$	$c_{\mathrm{ii\_inhib}} = 20$
$c_{\mathrm{iw\_ColorColor}} = 0.005$	$c_{\mathrm{iw\_ColorColor}} = 0.3$
$c_{\mathrm{iw\_ColorShape}} = 0.0025$	$c_{\mathrm{iw\_ColorShape}} = 0.001$
$c_{\mathrm{iw\_ShapeShape}} = 0.005$	$c_{\mathrm{iw\_ShapeShape}} = 0.3$
$c_{\mathrm{iw\_ShapeColor}} = 0.0025$	$c_{\mathrm{iw\_ShapeColor}} = 0.001$
$c_{\mathrm{wi\_ColorColor}} = 1$	$c_{\mathrm{wi\_ColorColor}} = 3$
$c_{\mathrm{wi\_ColorShape}} = .5$	$c_{\mathrm{wi\_ColorShape}} = 0.1$
$c_{\mathrm{wi\_ShapeShape}} = 1$	$c_{\mathrm{wi\_ShapeShape}} = 3$
$c_{\mathrm{wi\_ShapeColor}} = 0.5$	$c_{\mathrm{wi\_ShapeColor}} = 0.1$

$$\tau \dot{i}_{\text{color}}(t) = -i_{\text{color}}(t) + h_{i_{\text{color}}} + S_{i_{\text{color}}}(t) + c_{ii_{\text{excite}}} \Lambda(i_{\text{color}}(t))$$
$$- c_{ii_{\text{inhib}}} \Lambda(i_{\text{shape}}(t)) + c_{iw_{\text{ColorShape}}} \sum \sum \Lambda(w_{f2}(t)) \qquad (13)$$
$$+ c_{iw_{\text{ColorColor}}} \sum \sum \Lambda(w_{f1}(t))$$

ACKNOWLEDGEMENTS

The authors thank the parents and children who participated in this research. We also thank Gregor Schöner, Sammy Perone, Jeff Johnson, and Vanessa Simmering for critical discussions as we developed the dynamic neural field model, as well as undergraduate members of the SPAM Lab for their assistance with data collection. This work was supported by National Institutes of Health R01-MH062480 and National Science Foundation BCS-1029082 awarded to J.P.S.

MODELING THE EMERGENT EXECUTIVE: IMPLICATIONS FOR THE STRUCTURE AND DEVELOPMENT OF EXECUTIVE FUNCTION

Sandra A. Wiebe

ABSTRACT In this *Monograph*, Buss and Spencer develop a novel theory of preschool executive function (EF) based on the principles of dynamic systems theory (DST). In this commentary, I discuss how this model contributes to our understanding of EF and highlight challenges that remain to be addressed. First, I discuss Buss and Spencer's model in the context of existing theories, and in terms of the processes thought to underlie developmental improvements in card-sorting. Next, I explore implications for our understanding of the structure of EF in early childhood. Finally, I suggest possible extensions of this approach to later development, including whether and how this work might shed light on relations between individual differences in early EF and later developmental outcomes.

In this *Monograph*, Buss and Spencer set out to develop a theory of executive function (EF) in early childhood. Early childhood is of interest because it is marked by rapid growth in the ability to regulate behavior, both in the laboratory setting (Jones, Rothbart, & Posner, 2003) and in children's everyday lives (Moilanen, Shaw, Dishion, Gardner, & Wilson, 2009). Gains at the behavioral level are accompanied by, and thought to depend on, key milestones in brain development, including the dynamic overproduction and pruning of synapses in the frontal lobes and progressive increases in gray and white matter volumes (Huttenlocher & Dabholkar, 1997; Lenroot & Giedd, 2006). Hughes (2002) suggested that studying EF in early childhood can provide unique insights into its nature and development because the

---

Corresponding author: Sandra Wiebe, Department of Psychology, University of Alberta, P217 Biological Sciences Building, Edmonton, AB T6G 2E9, Canada, email: sandra.wiebe@ualberta.ca

construct may in fact be observed in a purer form than later in development, when more complex and less easily interpretable tasks are needed.

As an initial step in theory development, Buss and Spencer choose to focus on the dimensional change card sorting task (DCCS). This task was developed nearly two decades ago (Zelazo, Frye, & Rapus, 1996), and it has arguably become the prototypical measure of early childhood EF, as evidenced by a substantial body of literature using this task including a previous SRCD monograph (Zelazo, Müller, Frye, & Marcovitch, 2003). Carlson (2003) suggested that the DCCS could serve as a marker task of frontal lobe development in early childhood. Notably, several prominent theories already claim to explain what underlies children's difficulties with shifting between alternative ways to classify multidimensional stimuli (Kirkham, Cruess, & Diamond, 2003; Morton & Munakata, 2002; Perner & Lang, 2002; Zelazo et al., 2003). Buss and Spencer are thus faced with the task of arguing that that their theory outperforms existing theories, explaining previously documented experimental effects on the DCCS and generating novel predictions.

Buss and Spencer approach this challenge from the perspective of dynamic systems theory (DST), a meta-theoretical approach that seeks to explain the emergence of new behaviors through the interaction of multiple factors across multiple timescales, conceptualizing the developing person as a self-organizing system (Thelen & Smith, 2006). DST seems particularly well-matched to the task of explaining preschoolers' emergent ability to flexibly shift their attention because of DST theorists' previous success in applying this approach to another example of perseveration in early development, namely, the A-not-B error. Thelen, Schöner, Scheier, and Smith (2001) successfully modeled seemingly disparate features of the A-not-B perseverative reaching error, and contexts under which it was or was not observed, in a dynamic field theory model that was elegant in its simplicity, where "younger" and "older" models differed in their ability to sustain activation at a particular location after perceptual input ceased.

Buss and Spencer aim to accomplish the same feat for the DCCS. They do so by creating a dynamic neural field (DNF) model, which is grounded in DST but also incorporates current evidence about the organizing principles of neural networks. This model largely succeeds in replicating children's patterns of performance on a broad cross-section of DCCS variants that have been developed by previous researchers. In their model, perseveration and successful shifting are byproducts of interactions between multiple network fields coding different types of information, such that the "mature" model achieves cognitive flexibility without resorting to a homunculus-like central controller. To support their argument that their model adds value over existing approaches, Buss and Spencer do not simply account for existing findings, but use their model to generate several novel hypotheses based on

105

the proposal that binding of multidimensional representations of stimuli, and empirical tests broadly support these predictions.

In this commentary, I first discuss how this *Monograph*'s findings add to our understanding of the processes underlying developmental improvements on the DCCS. I then turn to implications for ideas about the structure of EF in early childhood, a topic of recent interest and perhaps controversy. Finally, I suggest several possible implications this work has for the development of EF *after* the period of early childhood.

EMERGENT EF: WHAT DEVELOPS?

Buss and Spencer begin the *Monograph* with a comprehensive review of existing theories that have attempted to explain the decline of perseveration and the emergence of successful switching on the DCCS. Some theorists have attributed developmental change to the emergence of new cognitive abilities, such that older children's approach to the DCCS is qualitatively different from that of younger children. For example, both the original and revised forms of Zelazo's cognitive complexity and control (CCC/CCC-r) theory posit that children must develop the capacity to represent and reflect on a nested structure of if-then rules in order to succeed on the DCCS (Zelazo & Frye, 1998; Zelazo et al., 2003). Alternatively, Perner and colleagues have emphasized the need to recognize that the same object can be described in more than one way (Kloo & Perner, 2005; Perner & Lang, 2002). These theories hold that young preschoolers are fundamentally incapable of grasping what is required of them by the DCCS, leading them to continue responding based on what they know, hence responding perseveratively.

Others have sought to explain improvements in DCCS performance on the basis of quantitative change. Kirkham et al. (2003) suggested that when attention is directed to a dimension of a stimulus, it acquires the property of inertia such that force is required to redirect it to another dimension, and children's success at switching is dependent on their having sufficient inhibitory capacity to overcome this attentional inertia. Morton and Munakata (2002) likewise recognize the central role of the previously relevant dimension, but consider this information to be held in the system in the form of a latent trace. They attribute the achievement of the ability to shift to improvements in the ability to actively maintain activation of the postswitch rule in working memory *without* directed inhibition of the preswitch rule, although in their neural network model, suppression of the no-longer-relevant rule is achieved indirectly via lateral inhibitory connections. Notably, both of these accounts attribute success on the DCCS to maturation of prefrontal cortex, a suggestion that is consistent with neuroimaging findings (Moriguchi & Hiraki, 2009).

Buss and Spencer's DNF model falls squarely within the latter camp, as they account for perseveration and switching within the same model, by changing several model parameters. As Buss and Spencer acknowledge, their model shares several important features with that of Morton and Munakata (2002). In both models, the key element driving perseveration in younger children is competition between memory traces from preswitch and postswitch trials, which creates conflict leading to perseveration if not resolved appropriately. Hebbian learning results in activation of the preswitch dimension carrying over into the second phase of the game, and developmental improvements are rooted in better ability to maintain activation of the postswitch rule in top-down, "prefrontal" components of the model.

However, Buss and Spencer's DNF model also incorporates novel features that allow them to replicate a broader cross-section of empirical findings involving variants of the DCCS. A central feature of their model is its architecture, which uses spatial coding to bind color and shape properties of stimuli. Consequently, the model not only learns about the rule, but also learns about the specific color and shape values used in the task *and* their spatial placement. These learned associations also carry forward and may compete or cooperate with the relevant mappings in the postswitch phase, helping or hindering the model's ability to sort cards in the postswitch phase. The role of spatial information in their model forms the basis of a novel prediction, namely, that simply moving the cards between the pre- and post-switch phases has the potential to change children's performance on the DCCS by increasing or decreasing conflict. Children's improved performance in the Negative Priming condition and impaired performance in the No-Conflict Negative Priming condition align fairly closely with the DNF model's predictions. Because the same manipulation (moving the cards) had opposite effects on children's level of performance depending on the task configuration, it seems unlikely that moving the cards between the pre- and post-switch phases was effective because it made the transition more salient, another manipulation that has been found to help children avoid perseveration in the DCCS (Mack, 2007).

Furthermore, patterns of model activation suggest that conflict and cooperation between dimensions occur and influence task performance not only in the post-switch phase of the DCCS, but also in the pre-switch phase. This is particularly evident in a version of the DCCS where the salience of one dimension is decreased, but presumably applies to other versions as well. Studies of neural correlates have likewise found that children who succeed in the task differ from children who perseverate in both pre- and post-switch phases: Success is associated with greater prefrontal activation and smaller N2 event-related potentials—related to conflict processing—whereas perseveration is linked to the opposite pattern (Espinet, Anderson, & Zelazo, 2012; Moriguchi & Hiraki, 2009).

Buss and Spencer take a clear position on *what* changes over the course of EF development in early childhood. However, it is less clear *how* EF changes over time, as the question of change over time is not dealt with in the current set of simulations, and differences between the "younger" and "older" model parameters were selected manually. Because of the bimodal nature of children's performance on the post-switch phase of the DCCS—they either get it or they don't—any attempt to model change over time must capture this developmental discontinuity (van Bers, Visser, van Schijndel, Mandell, & Raijmakers, 2011). The simulations presented in this *Monograph* successfully model this pass-fail pattern of performance by selecting separate distributions of model parameters to represent groups of younger and older children. It appears that this process took some care, as some parameter combinations had to be rejected because they produced intermediate levels of post-switch performance; this suggests that developing a model capturing how children move from perseveration to successful performance could face some challenges.

Buss and Spencer speculate that Hebbian learning mechanisms might be sufficient to shape the organization of the dimensional attention system and increase its selectivity as specified by their theory. They suggest that daily experiences such as language learning might help children build representations of relevant dimensions to which they ought to attend. These ideas bring to mind research on the pruning and sculpting of synapses in the prefrontal cortex during this time period (e.g., Huttenlocher & Dabholkar, 1997), and raise questions about the degree to which experience can shape these processes. Some have suggested that the protracted development of prefrontal cortex makes it more open to environmental influences, both enriching and detrimental (Bull, Espy, Wiebe, Sheffield, & Nelson, 2011; Raver, McCoy, Lowenstein, & Pess, 2013). Testing this hypothesis could be a fruitful area of exploration for modelers, with clear implications for understanding and improving interventions to improve children's EF skills.

DEFINING THE STRUCTURE OF EMERGENT EF

The stated larger goal of this *Monograph* is to develop a theoretical approach that informs not only our understanding of children's performance on the DCCS, important as that task may be, but also speaks to conceptualization of EF as a construct. EF is commonly defined as a set of distinct higher level processes that work together to enable goal-directed behavior, most commonly including the ability to maintain and update information in working memory, to inhibit prepotent responses, and to shift attentional or response sets (Garon, Bryson, & Smith, 2008; Miyake et al., 2000). Buss and Spencer use this EF framework to organize their review of the literature examining the role of specific EF components in DCCS performance. Given the diversity of theoretical viewpoints seeking to explain the requirements of the DCCS, it is unsurprising that there is also disagreement regarding the precise components of EF tapped by the DCCS. Some researchers have used the task as an index of children's set shifting abilities (e.g., Moriguchi & Hiraki, 2009), whereas others have categorized it as a measure of inhibitory control (e.g., Best & Miller, 2010). Garon et al. (2008) argued that children's successful performance on the DCCS exemplifies all three components of EF: children must keep the current rule in mind, shift their attention from color to shape or vice versa in the second phase of the game, and restrain themselves from continuing to respond according to the old rule when it no longer applies.

However, there is reason to question the divisions among EF components as they apply to early development. This evidence comes from studies using the latent variable approach, which attempts to parse the structure of EF by analyzing patterns of correlation across tasks thought to assess different aspects of EF rather than manipulating demands within the same task (Miyake et al., 2000). In studies using this approach, participants complete a battery of tasks selected to assess the constructs of interest (e.g., inhibition, working memory, and shifting). Structural equation modeling (SEM) is used to test whether the pattern of associations among tasks is consistent with that implied by the model, and that it cannot be explained equally well by a more parsimonious model. For example, if the three-factor model of EF is supported, there should be greater overlap in variance among tasks assessing the same EF component than between tasks assessing different components. The latent variable approach is particularly well-suited to the study of EF because of the task impurity problem, namely, that performance on any EF task reflects variability in both the control processes of interest and in processes related to other abilities required to complete the task, such as language or motor skills (Miyake et al., 2000). Latent EF can be measured very reliably even in early childhood, whereas individual tasks often demonstrate unacceptably low reliability (Willoughby & Blair, 2011).

When applied to samples of older children and adults, the latent variable approach has supported a multifactor structure with substantial correlations between factors (Lehto, Juujarvi, Kooistra, & Pulkkinen, 2003; McAuley & White, 2011; Miyake et al., 2000). However, a different picture has emerged in early childhood, the developmental period that Buss and Spencer seek to capture in this *Monograph*. In preschool children, a single-factor model of EF typically fits the data as well as less parsimonious, multicomponent models. This finding has been most consistently replicated in 3-year-old (Wiebe et al., 2011; Willoughby, Wirth, & Blair, 2012), although several studies have found similar findings in older preschool children (Wiebe, Espy, & Charak, 2008; Willoughby, Blair, Wirth, Greenberg, & FLP Investigators, 2010); however, see Miller, Giesbrecht, Müller, McInerney, & Kerns, 2012, for an exception). This body of literature calls into question the notion that EF components are clearly distinguishable in early childhood, prompting the suggestion that EF undergoes differentiation over the course of development (Shing, Lindenberger, Diamond, Li, & Davidson, 2010). It should be noted, however, that most studies using this approach have included only measures of inhibition and working memory. Miller and colleagues (2012) included tasks selected to measure set shifting—including the DCCS—but ultimately used these tasks as additional indicators of their working memory factor because shifting and working memory were so highly correlated as to create problems with model estimation.

Although SEM and computational modeling are fundamentally different approaches to studying the structure of EF, SEM findings can be informed by Buss and Spencer's work in the present *Monograph* and previous work by Munakata and her colleagues. Buss and Spencer describe recent and ongoing efforts to use the DFT framework to develop models of tasks developed to test response inhibition, working memory, and set shifting within the same framework. They suggest that this work could help us understand the processes that give rise to the typical 3-factor structure commonly supported in SEM studies of older children and adults (Lehto et al., 2003; Miyake et al., 2000). I believe this approach can also provide insight into the apparent unity of EF when assessed in early childhood. When presented with patterns of input, "younger" and "older" models respond in ways that, in children, would be interpreted as reflecting variability in working memory, inhibitory control, and shifting abilities, and it is tempting to ascribe these abilities to separable modules. However, the DNF model lacks any such structures; rather, patterns of responding that look like the model is holding a rule in mind, inhibiting a prepotent response, or shifting attentional set are all emergent properties of the same model architecture, such that selectively boosting the activation of the color field inhibits competing activation in the shape field, resulting in successful switching. Given that the latent variable approach is rooted in patterns of correlation, if the ability to maintain information in working memory and to inhibit competing alternatives are coupled at a fundamental level, it seems logical that patterns of covariance among tasks that require either of these abilities converge on a single factor. Perhaps, by developing DFT models of common preschool EF tasks, researchers can determine why preschool EF typically appears less complex, and even model the transition to more complex EF structures in later development.

EMERGENT EF AND LATER DEVELOPMENT

Although the focus of this *Monograph* is on EF in early childhood, Buss and Spencer frame their model as the starting point for a more comprehensive theory. Given that substantial EF development takes place between age 5 and adulthood (Best & Miller, 2010; Davidson, Amso, Anderson, & Diamond, 2006; Shing et al., 2010), a natural question is how their work might inform our understanding of later development—in EF and in other domains with demonstrated connections to EF.

First, how does Buss and Spencer's DFT model extend to later developments in set shifting? The DCCS differs in important ways from card-sorting tasks used to examine set shifting in older children and adults. In typical assessments of task-switching, participants must hold multiple rules in mind, as participants must select among several possible stimulus-response mappings when responding to each stimulus, guided by a cue that specifies which of several dimensions is relevant on that trial; in the DCCS, children must suppress the first rule when the second rule is introduced. By age 5, children are able to succeed on simple versions of task-switching paradigms such as the Advanced DCCS (Zelazo, 2006) and the Shape School task (Espy, 1997). In the Wisconsin Card Sorting Test (WCST; Grant & Berg, 1948), adults must deduce which of several rules is correct on the basis of feedback on their performance, whereas the rule is taught explicitly in the DCCS. Young children tend to perseverate at high rates on the WCST and do not exhibit adult-like performance until roughly age 10 (Chelune & Baer, 1986).

Extension of the modeling approach described in this *Monograph* to more complex card-sorting tasks seems like a natural next step, and would allow the exploration of many interesting questions. In tackling this later period in development, will quantitative change be sufficient as the present *Monograph* suggests is the case in early childhood, or will it be necessary to incorporate qualitative change? Some have explained apparent qualitative differences in set shifting across development in terms of quantitative change in EF components (Davidson et al., 2006), whereas others have argued for qualitative changes at the neurobehavioral level (Chatham, Frank, & Munakata, 2009; Chevalier, Huber, Wiebe, & Espy, 2013). For example, in a recent study comparing 5-year olds', 10-year olds', and adults' performance on a computerized task-switching paradigm, younger children benefited significantly from a transition cue that explicitly tells them when they need to switch, suggesting that by default they did not "plan ahead" for the possibility of a switch but instead reacted to each cue after it appears. Older children and adults, on the other hand, were paradoxically hindered in their performance by transition cues, which was interpreted as a sign that they were using bottom-up perceptual mismatch between successive trials as a cue that an attentional shift was necessary (Chevalier et al., 2013).

Second, can DFT modeling inform our understanding of how and why EF in early childhood predicts later outcomes in many domains? Buss and Spencer suggest that preschool EF is an important topic because of its link to later developmental outcomes, including academic performance, externalizing problems, and health behavior; these findings are drawn from research on individual differences, where variability in children's task performance is taken to reflect meaningful variation in EF. However, the experiments reviewed and replicated in the present *Monograph* take an experimental approach to studying EF, where task demands are manipulated to isolate the processes involved in task performance, for example, by manipulating the degree of conflict between response options; within this perspective, interindividual variability is typically conceptualized "noise." These approaches should be complementary, because a better understanding of EF is necessary if to understand its relations with other constructs.

As already discussed, the DNF model provides important insight into the relation between DCCS task performance and the abilities that contribute to EF. It is generally recognized that, although DCCS performance is bimodal, underlying EF skills—or model parameters—are graded. As such, any one version of the DCCS can provide only limited information about a child's true EF abilities. Although success on the standard DCCS is often viewed as a significant milestone in EF development, it seems unlikely that this version of the task is privileged as an index of prefrontal maturation, making this achievement somewhat arbitrary. To use the DCCS to measure a child's EF capabilities with sensitivity, the best approach might be to "triangulate" by testing performance under a variety of conditions with varying task demands. In fact, Carlson (2012) does something very similar in her recently developed EF scale, which is based on the DCCS but incorporates simpler levels (e.g., intradimensional shifts) and more advanced levels (e.g., the advanced DCCS). The DNF model clearly has implications for EF measurement, and as Buss and Spencer extend this approach to capture a wider range of EF tasks and periods of development its relevance will increase. It is less evident how this approach could be applied to capture the mechanisms whereby EF supports development in other domains, but if successful, this would be an important future direction.

CONCLUSION

In this *Monograph*, Buss and Spencer draw on principles of DST to propose a novel theory of EF in early childhood that, rather than relying on homuncular top-down control, accomplishes rule-based card-sorting via an emergent collective that "is softly-assembled 'in the moment'" (p. 90). The authors develop and test a set of models that replicate younger and older preschool children's responses to DCCS variants differing in the degree and type of conflict between representations formed before and after the rule switch. Their approach is unique in that it posits a role for spatial coding; this suggestion is supported by behavioral data from a new variant of the DCCS. Buss and Spencer's achievement is impressive in that their theory appears to hold its own in a field already crowded with theoretical perspectives. That said, ultimately the DNF model of the DCCS described in this *Monograph* might best be viewed as an initial step and proof of concept in the process of developing a comprehensive theory of EF and its development.

REFERENCES

Best, J. R., & Miller, P. H. (2010). A developmental perspective on executive function. *Child Development*, **81**(6), 1641–1660. doi: 10.1111/j.1467-8624.2010.01499.x

Bull, R., Espy, K. A., Wiebe, S. A., Sheffield, T. D., & Nelson, J. M. (2011). Using confirmatory factor analysis to understand executive control in preschool children: Sources of variation in emergent mathematic achievement. *Developmental Science*, **14**(4), 679–692. doi: 10.1111/j.1467-7687.2010.01012.x

Carlson, S. M. (2003). Executive function in context: Development, measurement, theory, and experience [Commentary on "The development of executive function in early childhood," by P.D. Zelazo, U. Muller, D. Frye, & S. Marcovitch]. *Monographs of the Society for Research in Child Development*, **68**(3), 138–151. doi: 10.1111/j.1540-5834.2003.06803012.x

Carlson, S. M. (2012, June). A graded measure of executive function for preschool children. In J. A. Griffin (Chair), *Developing New Measures to Assess the School Readiness of Young Children: The Interagency Consortium for School Readiness Outcome Measures*. Head Start's 11th National Research Conference, Washington, DC.

Chatham, C. H., Frank, M. J., & Munakata, Y. (2009). Pupillometric and behavioral markers of a developmental shift in the temporal dynamics of cognitive control. *Proceedings of the National Academy of Sciences of the United States of America*, **106**(14), 5529–5533. doi: 10.1073/pnas.0810002106

Chelune, G. J., & Baer, R. A. (1986). Developmental norms for the Wisconsin Card Sorting Test. *Journal of Clinical and Experimental Neuropsychology*, **8**(3), 219–228. doi: 10.1080/01688638608401314

Chevalier, N., Huber, K. L., Wiebe, S. A., & Espy, K. A. (2013). Qualitative change in executive control during childhood and adulthood. *Cognition*, **128**(1), 1–12. doi: 10.1016/j.cognition.2013.02.012

Davidson, M. C., Amso, D., Anderson, L. C., & Diamond, A. (2006). Development of cognitive control and executive functions from 4 to 13 years: Evidence from manipulations of memory, inhibition, and task switching. *Neuropsychologia*, **44**(11), 2037–2078. doi: 10.1016/j.neuropsychologia.2006.02.006

Espinet, S. D., Anderson, J. E., & Zelazo, P. D. (2012). N2 amplitude as a neural marker of executive function in young children: An ERP study of children who switch versus perseverate on the Dimensional Change Card Sort. *Developmental Cognitive Neuroscience*, **2S**, S49–S58. doi: 10.1016/j.dcn.2011.12.002

Espy, K. A. (1997). The Shape School: Assessing executive function in preschool children. *Developmental Neuropsychology*, **13**(4), 495–499.

Garon, N., Bryson, S. E., & Smith, I. M. (2008). Executive function in preschoolers: A review using an integrative framework. *Psychological Bulletin*, **134**(1), 31–60. doi: 10.1037/0033-2909.134.1.31

Grant, D. A., & Berg, E. A. (1948). A behavioral analysis of degree of reinforcement and ease of shifting to new responses in a Weigl-type card-sorting problem. *Journal of Experimental Psychology*, **38**(4), 404–411. doi: 10.1037/h0059831

Hughes, C. (2002). Executive functions and development: Why the interest? *Infant and Child Development*, **11**(2), 69–71. doi: 10.1002/icd.296

Huttenlocher, P. R., & Dabholkar, A. S. (1997). Regional differences in synaptogenesis in human cerebral cortex. *The Journal of Comparative Neurology*, **387**(2), 167–178. doi: 10.1002/(SICI)1096-9861(19971020)387:2<167::AID-CNE1>3.0.CO;2-Z

Jones, L. B., Rothbart, M. K., & Posner, M. I. (2003). Development of executive attention in preschool children. *Developmental Science*, **6**(5), 498–504. doi: 10.1111/1467-7687.00307

Kirkham, N. Z., Cruess, L., & Diamond, A. (2003). Helping children apply their knowledge to their behavior on a dimension-switching task. *Developmental Science*, **6**(5), 449–468. doi: 10.1111/1467-7687.00300

Kloo, D., & Perner, J. (2005). Disentangling dimensions in the dimensional change card-sorting task. *Developmental Science*, **8**(1), 44–56. doi: 10.1111/j.1467-7687.2005.00392.x

Lehto, J. E., Juujarvi, P., Kooistra, L., & Pulkkinen, L. (2003). Dimensions of executive functioning: Evidence from children. *British Journal of Developmental Psychology*, **21**, 59–80. doi: 10.1348/026151003321164627

Lenroot, R. K., & Giedd, J. N. (2006). Brain development in children and adolescents: Insights from anatomical magnetic resonance imaging. *Neuroscience and Biobehavioral Reviews*, **30**(6), 718–729. doi: 10.1016/j.neubiorev.2006.06.001

Mack, W. (2007). Improving postswitch performance in the dimensional change card-sorting task: The importance of the switch and of pretraining by redescribing the test cards. *Journal of Experimental Child Psychology*, **98**(4), 243–251. doi: 10.1016/j.jecp.2007.05.004

McAuley, T., & White, D. A. (2011). A latent variables examination of processing speed, response inhibition, and working memory during typical development. *Journal of Experimental Child Psychology*, **108**(3), 453–468. doi: 10.1016/j.jecp.2010.08.009

Miller, M. R., Giesbrecht, G. F., Müller, U., McInerney, R. J., & Kerns, K. A. (2012). A latent variable approach to determining the structure of executive function in preschool children. *Journal of Cognition and Development*, **13**(3), 395–423. doi: 10.1080/15248372.2011.585478

Miyake, A., Friedman, N. P., Emerson, M. J., Witzki, A. H., Howerter, A., & Wager, T. D. (2000). The unity and diversity of executive functions and their contributions to complex "frontal lobe" tasks: A latent variable analysis. *Cognitive Psychology*, **41**(1), 49–100. doi: 10.1006/cogp.1999.0734

Moilanen, K. L., Shaw, D. S., Dishion, T. J., Gardner, F., & Wilson, M. (2009). Predictors of longitudinal growth in inhibitory control in early childhood. *Social Development*, **19**(2), 326–347. doi: 10.1111/j.1467-9507.2009.00536.x

Moriguchi, Y., & Hiraki, K. (2009). Neural origin of cognitive shifting in young children. *Proceedings of the National Academy of Sciences*, **106**(14), 6017–6021. doi: 10.1073/pnas.0809747106

Morton, J. B., & Munakata, Y. (2002). Active versus latent representations: A neural network model of perseveration, dissociation, and decalage. *Developmental Psychobiology*, **40**, 255–265. doi: 10.1002/dev.10033

Perner, J., & Lang, B. (2002). What causes 3-year-olds' difficulty on the dimensional change card sorting task? *Infant and Child Development*, **11**(2), 93–105. doi: 10.1002/icd.299

Raver, C. C., McCoy, D. C., Lowenstein, A. E., & Pess, R. (2013). Predicting individual differences in low-income children's executive control from early to middle childhood. *Developmental Science*, **16**(3), 394–408. doi: 10.1111/desc.12027

Shing, Y. L., Lindenberger, U., Diamond, A., Li, S-. C., & Davidson, M. C. (2010). Memory maintenance and inhibitory control differentiate from early childhood to adolescence. *Developmental Neuropsychology*, **35**(6), 679–697. doi: 10.1080/87565641.2010.508546

Thelen, E., Schöner, G., Scheier, C., & Smith, L. B. (2001). The dynamics of embodiment: A field theory of infant perseverative reaching. *Behavioral and Brain Sciences*, **24**, 1–86. doi: 10.1017/S0140525X01003910

Thelen, E., & Smith, L. B. (2006). Dynamic systems theory. In: W. Damon, & R. M. Lerner (Eds.), *Handbook of child psychology. Volume 1: Theoretical models of human development* (6th ed., pp. 258–312). Hoboken, NJ: Wiley.

Van Bers, B. M. C. W., Visser, I., van Schijndel, T. J. P., Mandell, D. J., & Raijmakers, M. E. J. (2011). The dynamics of development on the dimensional change card sorting task. *Developmental Science*, **14**(5), 960–971. doi: 10.1111/j.1467-7687.2011.01045.x

Wiebe, S. A., Espy, K. A., & Charak, D. (2008). Using confirmatory factor analysis to understand executive control in preschool children: I. Latent structure. *Developmental Psychology*, **44**(2), 575–587. doi: 10.1037/0012-1649.44.2.575

Wiebe, S. A., Sheffield, T., Nelson, J. M., Clark, C. A. C., Chevalier, N., & Espy, K. A. (2011). The structure of executive function in 3-year-olds. *Journal of Experimental Child Psychology*, **108**(3), 436–452. doi: 10.1016/j.jecp.2010.08.008

Willoughby, M. T., & Blair, C. B. (2011). Test-retest reliability of a new executive function battery for use in early childhood. *Child Neuropsychology*, **17**(6), 564–579. doi: 10.1080/09297049.2011.554390

Willoughby, M. T., Blair, C. B., Wirth, R. J., Greenberg, M., & FLP Investigators. (2010). The measurement of executive function at age 3 years: Psychometric properties and criterion validity of a new battery of tasks. *Psychological Assessment*, **22**(2), 306–317. doi: 10.1037/a0018708

Willoughby, M. T., Wirth, R. J., & Blair, C. B. (2012). Executive function in early childhood: Longitudinal measurement invariance and developmental change. *Psychological Assessment*, **24**(2), 418–431. doi: 10.1037/a0025779

Zelazo, P. D. (2006). The Dimensional Change Card Sort (DCCS): A method of assessing executive function in children. *Nature Protocols*, **1**(1), 297–301. doi: 10.1038/nprot.2006.46

Zelazo, P. D., & Frye, D. (1998). Cognitive complexity and control: II. The development of executive function in childhood. *Current Directions in Psychological Science*, **7**(4), 121–126. doi: 10.1111/1467-8721.ep10774761

Zelazo, P. D., Frye, D., & Rapus, T. (1996). An age-related dissociation between knowing rules and using them. *Cognitive Development*, **11**, 37–63. doi: 10.1016/S0885-2014%2896%2990027-1

Zelazo, P. D., Müller, U., Frye, D., & Marcovitch, S. (2003). The development of executive function in early childhood. *Monographs of the Society for Research in Child Development*, **68**(3), 1–137. doi: 10.1111/j.1540-5834.2003.06803001.x

COMMENTARY

DYNAMIC FIELD THEORY AND EXECUTIVE FUNCTIONS: LENDING EXPLANATION TO CURRENT THEORIES OF DEVELOPMENT

J. Bruce Morton

ABSTRACT Buss and Spencer's monograph is an impressive achievement that is sure to have a lasting impact on the field of child development. The dynamic field theory (DFT) model, that forms the heart of this contribution, is ambitious in scope, detailed in its implementation, and rigorously tested against data, old and new. As such, the ideas contained in this fine document represent a qualitative advance in our understanding of young children's behavior, and lay a foundation for future research into the developmental origins of executive functioning.

My 4-year-old daughter is very proud of herself—she has learned to ride her two-wheel bike. A few weeks ago, she was very eager to try, so we took her and her bike to a nearby baseball diamond and helped her up onto the seat. She was a bit wobbly at first, but quickly found her balance and got going round and round the diamond on her own, unassisted. She giggled with delight. It was a truly joyous moment. Still, despite her impressive progress, she can't quite ride like her older brother—starting at will, riding consistently straight, stopping at corners, cognizant of cars, potholes, and pedestrians, and heeding the directives of her anxious parents. Put simply, she lacks control.

Inquiry into the psychological nature of control falls under the banner of the executive functions—processes that enable the planning, selection, initiation, stopping, and evaluation of voluntary actions. Executive functions (or EFs) operate on, but are not synonymous with, more elemental perceptual-motor capacities. My daughter, for example, has the necessary

Corresponding author: J. Bruce Morton, Ph.D., Associate Professor, Cognitive Development and Neuroimaging Laboratory, Department of Psychology, Brain and Mind Institute, Westminster Hall, 324, University of Western Ontario, London, ON N6A 3K7, Canada, email: jbrucemorton@gmail.com balance and strength to remain upright on her bike while turning the pedals—she has acquired a basic perceptual-motor skill. Over time though, this skill will (hopefully!) become more controlled. She will learn to plan different routes, adjust her speed given local changes in sidewalk traffic, brake at corners, stop signs, and street crossings, and monitor her turns to avoid painful spills. Adding control will not fundamentally change the mechanics of riding a bike—she will still need to keep her balance and turn the pedals. However, this ability will become subject to a variety of checks and balances and more finely adapted to the demands of her local environment. As such, a developing ability to control voluntary actions plays an indispensable role in my daughter's everyday experience.

Questions concerning the development of EF have enjoyed an enduring fascination, and for good reason. First, the basic phenomena elicited by EF tasks early in development are striking and counterintuitive. In the A-not-B task, for example, 7- to 12-month-old infants face an apparatus with two hiding wells, and watch as an attractive toy is hidden in one of the two wells, termed "A." Following a short delay, infants are allowed to search for the toy and most correctly search at A. Infants then watch as the toy is hidden in the second "B" well. Even though infants see the toy hidden at B, and begin searching only a few seconds later, most search at A. In short, they perseverate by showing persistent use of an old behavior when that behavior is no longer appropriate (Munakata, 1998). Long after they have mastered the A- not-B task, children will show a similar pattern of perseverative behavior in the Dimensional Change Card Sort task (or DCCS; Zelazo, 2006), the focus of this outstanding monograph. In the task, preschoolers sort test cards into bins marked with target cards. In the standard task, test cards match target cards only on a single dimension. Thus, children might sort red trucks and blue boats into bins marked with a blue truck and a red boat. In pre-switch trials, children sort the cards one way (e.g., by color), and typically do just fine. However, in post-switch trials, when they are instructed to switch and sort the cards in a new way (e.g., by shape), most 3.5-year-olds perseverate, by persistently sorting the cards the old way (i.e., by color). The phenomenon is all the more striking as it occurs despite children's apparent knowledge of the correct sorting rule. When asked where boats and trucks go in the new shape game, all children point to correct sorting trays. In spite of this, when asked to sort cards by shape, most 3-year-old children persist in sorting cards by color. The phenomenon is so striking observers are often left completely astounded. I remember administering a DCCS-like task to a young boy under the watchful eye of an older sibling. After perseverating on every post-switch trial, the boy stood up and proudly declared, "Wow, did you see that? I got them all right!" to which his incredulous older sibling replied, "No you didn't! You got them all wrong!" These kinds of counterintuitive behaviors are observed throughout early development and can be explained in terms of underdeveloped EF. In the A-not-B task, for example, infants persist in searching for the toy at A after watching the toy being hidden at B. While it is possible that infants forget seeing the toy hidden at B, clever experimentation has revealed that infants do in fact remember where the toy is. Their counterintuitive behavior thus appears to relate to problems withholding reaches to A. And in the DCCS, 3-year-olds correctly answer questions about new sorting rules, but persist in using old rules. Thus, early in development, simple behaviors like reaching and card sorting are intact but not subject to the regulatory checks and balances that ensure their seamless adaptation to the immediate environment.

A second reason for enduring interest in the development of EF is that individual differences in self-control assessed early in development longitudinally predict important psychological milestones. In one landmark series of studies, Walter Mischel showed that individual differences in young children's ability to forego small immediate rewards in lieu of larger future rewards predicted academic achievement, social adjustment, and coping skills 10 years later in adolescence. Subsequent investigations have indeed confirmed a close relationship between executive functioning skills and intellectual development, both in terms of school readiness and the rate of acquisition of skills such as math (Mischel, Shoda, & Peake, 1988). These data make sense: the ability to focus, hold relevant information in mind, and systematically test and evaluate possible solutions ought to impact how readily children master new intellectual and social challenges. And they do.

A third reason for enduring interest in the development of executive functioning concerns striking parallels between EF and brain development (Diamond, 2002). Broad-scale cortical networks associated with executive functions show continued functional and structural development into early adulthood, akin to the development of EF. Moreover, damage and/or dysfunction in these regions is associated with behaviors reminiscent of those observed in infants and young children. Patients who have undergone remedial lateral prefrontal resection, for example, show high rates of perseveration in card sorting tasks, much like 3.5-year-olds in the DCCS. And primates with experimentally induced lateral prefrontal lesions perseverate in object-search tasks, much like infants in the A-not-B task. Together, these data point to the possibility that the development of EF is related in a fundamental way to the development of particular cortical networks.

Tantalizing behavioral and neurophysiological evidence of this kind calls out for explanation and has contributed to sustained interest in understanding the development of EF. However, in spite of this, many basic issues remain unresolved. First, our understanding of the processes underlying EF remains highly provisional. The origins of this problem stems from the fact that EF, as the term is conventionally used, refers to functions—that is, things that follow from the implementation of a process. Planning is what follows from envisioning a future course of action. Response selection follows from the process of choosing one response over another. Behavioral inhibition follows the successful withholding of a behavior. And so on. The terms themselves are eloquent, and suggestive, but in the end, largely descriptive. They characterize the causal outcome of processes, but not the processes themselves. One approach to this problem has been to ask whether EF tasks—such as response inhibition tasks, working memory tasks, stimulus-response compatibility tasks, switching tasks, and so on—measure a single process or multiple processes. The answer is clear to a point—EF tasks do not appear to measure a single underlying process. Some analyses suggest three underlying processes—working memory, switching, and response inhibition (Miyake et al., 2000)while others suggest two (Hampshire, Parkin, Highfield, & Owen, 2012), with any single result depending in part on the number and type of tasks included in the original test battery, the number of participants included in the sample, and statistical interpretation. However, even if large-scale multivariate decompositions of different behavioral data sets were to converge on a similar set of underlying factors, we would still have only a provisional understanding of the underlying processes that give rise to the observed factor structure. We would be no closer to knowing what shared computation underlies different working memory tasks, for example, or how this computation differs from that underlying different switching tasks. Nor could we be certain that the observed factor structure reflects distinct components of EF. Resulting factors could conceivably be emergent properties of a highly dynamic complex system. Indeed, neuroimaging studies suggest working memory, response inhibition, and switching tasks utilize highly overlapping networks. Distinctions that appear real at a cognitive level of description seem to disappear when we switch to a neurophysiological level of description. These are challenging and fundamental problems that require a move beyond functional descriptions toward an explicit model of underlying computational mechanisms.

In a related vein, questions concerning the development of EF also remain largely unresolved. Foremost among these concern what develops and why. To date, developmentalists have relied heavily on traditional conceptualizations of EF, arguing, for example, that age-related changes in DCCS performance reflect underlying developments in inhibitory control and/or working memory, changes that are, in turn, linked to the maturation of certain brain regions, such as lateral prefrontal cortex. Explanations of this kind are valuable to a degree in that they provide a framework for organizing evidence and directing empirical inquiry. But they are also limited and limiting. First, they don't explain behaviors in terms that are much different than terms that describe the phenomena. To say, for example, that 3-year-olds who perseverate in DCCS fail to inhibit an old way of sorting is a perfectly apt description of their behavior. However, explaining the behavior in the same terms—that is, as a consequence of underdeveloped inhibition—does little to advance our understanding of perseveration. It simply restates the description in explanatory terms. To advance our understanding of behavior, we require explanations that appeal to concepts and/or mechanisms that are distinct from the behaviors being explained. Second, passing the burden of explanation over to a putative process such as brain maturation does more to obscure than illuminate. That the cortex changes dramatically over development is indisputable, as is the protracted development of the prefrontal cortex. Indeed, patterns of brain activity associated with switching, working memory, and inhibitory control change dramatically over development, as revealed by functional neuroimaging methods. However, as compelling as they are, these data are not explanatory. Patterns of brain activity revealed by fMRI say nothing more about process or mechanism than do accuracy or response time, precisely because neuroimaging and behavioral measures alike are simply correlates of unobservable cognitive operations. Thus, evidence that the development of certain brain regions proceeds in parallel with the development of EF does not offer, but requires explanation.

In summary then, questions concerning the development of EF have enjoyed an enduring interest among scholars of psychology for many years, but the field confronts sizable challenges conceptualizing the nature of these changes and their association with changes in brain structure and function. With this in mind, we can begin to appreciate the significance of Buss and Spencer's outstanding monograph. Focusing in particular on changes in behavior revealed by the DCCS task in the preschool years, Buss and Spencer present a computationally based account of EF development and its association with changes in cortical organization. Taking the structure of the human visual system as its point of departure, the dynamic field theory (DFT) model consists of separate perceptual fields that represent colors and shapes and whose activations, or representations, are bound together by a common spatial frame of reference. Activity in these fields is shaped by events in the world, such as the presentation of test cards in the DCCS, as well as prior experience, but is also subject to control via the biasing influence of a dimensional attention system. The model is important because it peels away the many layers of description that have been applied to EF and its development over the years and reveals the inner mechanics of the system. In short, it explains.

Consider, for example, perennial questions concerning the nature of EF. In the hands of Buss and Spencer's DFT model, descriptive characterizations of DCCS performance, such as those based on concepts of inhibition, give way to an explicit characterization of processing dynamics. Sorting by one feature of a test card leads, via incremental learning, to a preference for that feature in subsequent trials. Switching to a new feature therefore requires control, made possible by a biasing signal from the dimensional attention system. If the biasing signal is weak or incoherent, the model's preference for the first feature prevails, and the model perseverates. However, if the biasing signal is strong and coherent, the model switches to the new feature. This characterization of successes and failures in the DCCS goes beyond description and explains behavior in terms that are distinct from the phenomenon under consideration. The model makes explicit how processing might occur during task performance, so that we can begin to understand why rule switching might be associated with behavioral costs and lateral prefrontal cortex activity. Because on switch trials, activation to previously relevant features competes with activation to currently relevant features, the network requires added time to settle on a response, and does so only when top-down intervention sways the battle in favor of the currently relevant features. Thus, compared to repeat trials, responses on switch trials are slow and error prone, and place metabolic demands on the dimensional attention system.

Buss and Spencer's DFT model also provides clear, comprehensive explanation of observable changes in children's DCCS performance over the preschool years. Whereas standard developmental accounts appeal to descriptive concepts in place of detailed explanation, Buss and Spencer's DFT model links age-related change in DCCS performance to putative anatomical and physiological changes in the brain. The core of their account is that connections both within and between regions of the brain become stronger with development. These changes in turn have important consequences for the dynamics of larger systems and the capacity of the model to switch. Young models with weak connectivity have difficulty sustaining working memory like activations within fields and coherent interactions between fields. These models tend to perseverate when sorting criteria change. Older models with strong connectivity, by contrast, show sustained working memory like activity within fields and coherent interactions between fields. These models tend to switch when sorting criteria change. The importance of this account is that it explains age-related changes in DCCS performance in terms that are distinct from its description. Age-related changes in children's capacity to use new rules and inhibit old rules are explained with reference to a putative physiological mechanism as opposed to being turned around and offered up as explanation. While these ideas echo findings from previous modeling research, the current DFT model represents an enormous step forward in our understanding of the development of cognitive flexibility as revealed by the DCCS. First off, the model simulates an impressive set of extant behavioral effects, including performance in the canonical as well negative priming, training, full-change, partial-change, and relational complexity variants of the DCCS. This alone is impressive. But the model goes further, by making a number of predictions concerning the importance of space for DCCS performance that are not made by other theories. These predictions are tested and confirmed (Chapter 5). Taken together then, the work represented in this monograph is in a class of its own, both in its capacity to accommodate extant DCCS data and its capacity to direct new avenues of empirical inquiry.

The implications of Buss and Spencer's model for understanding brain-behavior associations and EF extend well beyond the DCCS though. The model, for example, forces a critical reexamination of switching, inhibition, and working memory as core processes underlying EF. Viewed from the standpoint of the model, switching is not a function computed by an isolated module, or a process that operates independently of inhibition and working memory. Instead, the capacity to switch emerges from a dynamic interplay of multiple fields whose activation is shaped by excitatory, inhibitory, and self-sustaining (or working memory-like) connections. Similarly, the model's capacity to inhibit sorting cards by color is an emergent property of coherent inputs to the color field from the dimensional attention system, as well as inhibitory connections between competing units in the color field. Viewed in this way, behaviors elicited by EF tasks are best thought of as emerging properties of a complex interacting system rather than direct measures of discrete underlying processes. Computational models, like Buss and Spencer's DFT model, are also indispensable for bridging the precarious divide between behavior and the brain. Contrary to popular opinion, neuroimaging methods do not provide a transparent window into the inner workings of the brain. They simply provide a physiological signal that rises and falls over time. The hard work of the cognitive neuroscientist is to explain why signal changes occur the way they do. The standard approach is to compare signal intensity during particular events, such as switch trials, with signal intensity during other events, such as repeat trials. Brain regions in which signal intensity changes across switch and repeat trials are then assumed to be functionally linked in some way with switching. The problem with this approach is that without an adequate characterization of what switching actually consists of, we can't say anything very specific about the function of brain regions associated with this operation. The importance of computational models is that they explicitly characterize unobservable cognitive operations so that we have a mechanistic characterization of what, for example, switching might consist of. Critically though, models generate quantitative predictors that can be used to model variability in physiological and behavioral measures. In a very real sense then, computational models provide a testable account of the unobservable cognitive processes that give rise to observed brain-behavior correlations.

As with any great theory, Buss and Spencer's model has limitations. Some of these call for refinements, others for deeper reflection. It is not clear, for example, how neurotransmission works in the model. It is well known that dopamine and its associated family of receptors play a central role in the function of EF networks, including prefrontal and cingulate cortices. And it is certainly possible to implement these details in models—in fact, models are ideally suited to simulating neuronal networks and their mode of neurotransmission (Frank, Seeberger, & O'Reilly, 2004). These details are noticeably absent in Buss and Spencer's DFT model. Second, the model, as presented, is largely isolated from a larger physical and social environment. The only event in the world the model is able to "comprehend" is the presentation of a test card in the DCCS. The model has no means of even knowing whether its responses are correct or incorrect, let alone whether its "world" is stable and supportive or chaotic and impoverished. While it was clearly not necessary to implement this degree of functionality in order to simulate age-related changes in DCCS performance, its absence limits the model's capacity to serve as a framework for understanding the origins of individual differences in EF early in development. As discussed earlier, individual differences in EF longitudinally predict important developmental milestones including academic achievement, social adjustment, and health-related behaviors. These individual differences are the product of both experiential (e.g., parenting, socioeconomic status, early life stress [Noble, McCandliss, & Farah, 2007]) and genetic (e.g., polymorphic variation, DNA methylation, chromatin remodeling) influences, although the nature of these effects and their possible interaction remain unclear. Computational models have great potential to help unravel these complex issues, but require mechanisms of neurotransmission and social-environmental interaction be specified in more detail than they are in Buss and Spencer's DFT model.

Limitations notwithstanding, Buss and Spencer's monograph is an impressive achievement that is sure to have a lasting impact on the field of child development. The DFT model that forms the heart of this contribution is ambitious in scope, detailed in its implementation, and rigorously tested against data, old and new. As such, the ideas contained in this fine document represent a qualitative advance in our understanding of young children's behavior, and lay a foundation for future research into the developmental origins of executive functioning.

REFERENCES

Diamond, A. (2002). Normal development of prefrontal cortex from birth to young adulthood: Cognitive functions, anatomy, and biochemistry. In D. T. Stuss & R. T. Knight (Eds.), *Principles of frontal lobe function* (406–503.). Oxford: Oxford University Press.

Frank, M. J., Seeberger, L. C., & O'Reilly, R. C. (2004). By carrot or by stick: Cognitive reinforcement learning in Parkinsonism. *Science*, **306**(5703), 1940–1943.

Hampshire, A., Parkin, B., Highfield, R., & Owen, A. M. (2012). Fractionating human intelligence. *Neuron*, **76**(6), 1–48.

Mischel, W., Shoda, Y., & Peake, P. K. (1988). The nature of adolescent competencies predicted by preschool delay of gratification. *Journal of Personality and Social Psychology*, **54**(4), 687–696.

Miyake, A., Friedman, N. P., Emerson, M. J., Witzki, A. H., Howerter, A., & Wager, T. D. (2000). The unity and diversity of executive functions and their contributions to complex "Frontal Lobe" tasks: A latent variable analysis. *Cognitive Psychology*, **41**(1), 49–100.

Munakata, Y. (1998). Infant perseveration and implications for object permanence theories: A PDP model of the AnotB task. *Developmental Science*, **1**(2), 161–211.

Noble, K. G., McCandliss, B. D., & Farah, M. J. (2007). Socioeconomic gradients predict individual differences in neurocognitive abilities. *Developmental Science*, **10**(4), 464–480.

Zelazo, P. D. (2006). The Dimensional Change Card Sort (DCCS): A method of assessing executive function in children. *Nat Protoc*, **1**(1), 297–301.

CONTRIBUTORS

Sandra A. Wiebe (Ph.D., University of Minnesota) is an Assistant Professor in the Department of Psychology at the University of Alberta. Her research uses behavioral and electrophysiological methods to examine the development of children's ability to regulate their thoughts, actions, and emotions in the early years, and the impact of environmental and genetic factors on these developing skills.

Dr. J. Bruce Morton is an Associate Professor of Psychology and core faculty member of the Brain and Mind Institute at the University of Western Ontario. His research focuses on inter-individual and developmental variability in cognitive control early in life.

Aaron T. Buss is an Assistant Professor of Psychology at the University of Tennessee. He received his Ph.D. from the University of Iowa in 2013. He is the recipient of the 2009 Simon Award and the 2013 Lewis Award from the University of Iowa.

John P. Spencer is a Professor of Psychology at The University of Iowa, the current director of the CHILDS Facility (CHild Imaging Laboratory in Developmental Science) and the founding Director of the Delta Center (Development and Learning from Theory to Application). He received a Sc.B. with Honors from Brown University in 1991 and a Ph.D. in Experimental Psychology from Indiana University in 1998. He is the recipient of the Irving J. Saltzman and the J.R. Kantor Graduate Awards from Indiana University, the 2003 Early Research Contributions Award from the Society for Research in Child Development, and the 2006 Robert L. Fantz Memorial Award from the American Psychological Foundation.

STATEMENT OF EDITORIAL POLICY

The SRCD *Monographs* series aims to publish major reports of developmental research that generates authoritative new findings and that foster a fresh perspective and/or integration of data/research on conceptually significant issues. Submissions may consist of individually or group-authored reports of findings from some single large-scale investigation or from a series of experiments centering on a particular question. Multiauthored sets of independent studies concerning the same underlying question also may be appropriate. A critical requirement in such instances is that the individual authors address common issues and that the contribution arising from the set as a whole be unique, substantial, and well integrated. Manuscripts reporting interdisciplinary or multidisciplinary research on significant developmental questions and those including evidence from diverse cultural, racial, and ethnic groups are of particular interest. Also of special interest are manuscripts that bridge basic and applied developmental science, and that reflect the international perspective of the Society. Because the aim of the *Monographs* series is to enhance cross-fertilization among disciplines or subfields as well as advance knowledge on specialized topics, the links between the specific issues under study and larger questions relating to developmental processes should emerge clearly and be apparent for both general readers and specialists on the topic. In short, irrespective of how it may be framed, work that contributes significant data and/or extends a developmental perspective will be considered.

Potential authors who may be unsure whether the manuscript they are planning wouldmake an appropriate submission to the SRCD *Monographs* are invited to draft an outline or prospectus of what they propose and send it to the incoming editor for review and comment.

Potential authors are not required to be members of the Society for Research in Child Development nor affiliated with the academic discipline of psychology to submit a manuscript for consideration by the *Monographs*. The significance of the work in extending developmental theory and in contributing new empirical information is the crucial consideration.

Submissions should contain a minimum of 80 manuscript pages (including tables and references). The upper boundary of 150–175 pages is more flexible, but authors should try to keep within this limit. Manuscripts must be double-spaced, 12pt Times New Roman font, with 1-inch margins. If color artwork is submitted, and the authors believe color art is necessary to the presentation of their work, the submissions letter should indicate that one or more authors or their institutions are prepared to pay the substantial costs associated with color art reproduction. Please submit manuscripts electronically to the SRCD *Monographs* Online Submissions and Review Site (Scholar One) at http://mc.manuscriptcentral.com/mono. Please contact the *Monographs* office with any questions at monographs@srcd.org.

The corresponding author for any manuscript must, in the submission letter, warrant that all coauthors are in agreement with the content of the manuscript. The corresponding author also is responsible for informing all coauthors, in a timely manner, of manuscript submission, editorial decisions, reviews received, and any revisions recommended. Before publication, the corresponding author must warrant in the submissions letter that the study has been conducted according to the ethical guidelines of the Society for Research in Child Development.

A more detailed description of all editorial policies, evaluation processes, and format requirements can be found under the "Submission Guidelines" link at http://srcd.org/publications/monographs.

Monographs Editorial Office
e-mail: monographs@srcd.org

Editor, Patricia J. Bauer
Department of Psychology, Emory University
36 Eagle Row
Atlanta, GA 30322
e-mail: pjbauer@emory.edu

Note to NIH Grantees

Pursuant to NIH mandate, Society through Wiley-Blackwell will post the accepted version of Contributions authored by NIH grantholders to PubMed Central upon acceptance. This accepted version will be made publicly available 12 months after publication. For further information, see http://www.wiley.com/go/nihmandate.

SUBJECT INDEX

Page numbers in *italics* refer to tables and figures.

CURRENT